church on
PURPOSE

Reinventing Discipleship, Community, & Justice

Adam L. Bond
Laura Mariko Cheifetz
Editors

Foreword by Aidsand F. Wright-Riggins III

JUDSON PRESS
PUBLISHERS SINCE 1824
VALLEY FORGE, PA

Judson Press has made every effort to trace the ownership of all quotes. In the event of a question arising from the use of a quote, we regret any error made and will be pleased to make the necessary correction in future printings and editions of this book.

Bible quotations in this volume are from the following:

Common English Bible © 2011 Common English Bible Used by permission. All rights reserved.

Complete Jewish Bible (CJB) Copyright © 1998 by David H. Stern. All rights reserved.

The Holy Bible, King James Version.

HOLY BIBLE, NEW INTERNATIONAL VERSION®. NIV®. Copyright © 1973, 1978, 1984, 2011 by Biblica, Inc.™ Used by permission. All rights reserved worldwide.

The New King James Version. Copyright © 1972, 1984 by Thomas Nelson Inc.

Holy Bible. New Living Translation copyright© 1996, 2004, 2007 by Tyndale House Foundation. Used by permission of Tyndale House Publishers, Inc. Carol Stream, Illinois 60188. All rights reserved.

New Revised Standard Version Bible, copyright © 1989, Division of Christian Education of the National Council of the Churches of Christ in the United States of America. Used by permission. All rights reserved.

Interior design by Crystal Devine.

Cover design by Wendy Ronga and Hampton Design Group.

Cataloging-in-Publication Data available upon request. Contact cip@judsonpress.com.

Printed in the U.S.A.

First printing, 2015.

Contents

PART I: REINVENTING DISCIPLESHIP

PART II: REINVENTING COMMUNITY

foreword

"FORWARD!" THIS IS THE CLARION CALL THAT THIS RACIALLY AND ethnically diverse group of 30- and 40-something-year-old women and men are calling the church toward. Their call is a gracious and engaging invitation to conversation about how the church of Jesus Christ may be reinvented, especially in the areas of discipleship, community, and justice. Adam Bond and Laura Mariko Cheifetz have assembled a team of talented and truth-telling ministry leaders who each beckon us to place a sign in front of our local church that reads, "Under Reconstruction."

As a denominational leader who has engaged with hundreds of churches and a thousand or so pastoral leaders over the course of my ministry, I have seen far too many churches that are stuck, stagnant, or stale, especially when it comes to being relevant to people twenty to thirty years younger than I. The way in which so many in my generation tell the story of Jesus, his love, and his plea that we develop as disciples, build community, and pursue justice doesn't seem to resonate as well to emerging generations.

As the parent of three adult children who are PK's (Preacher's Kids) and the live-in grandparent of a precocious PGK (Preacher's Grandkid), I often find myself bombarded by the kinds of concerns that are raised in this book: "How can I nurture a faith that is both personal and publically engaged and relevant?" "What does the Bible really have to say about such things as power, sex, and money?" "How might I share my faith without looking like a Bible-thumping, fighting fundamentalist?" "Can I really look to today's pulpit for authentic leadership and a word from God?" "How might the church satisfy my longing for a sense of community greater than what I find at the local gym and Starbucks?" "What do God and the church have to say about social inequality, environmental fragility, and my relationship with my non-Christian neighbor?" Is there a way to talk about church and being a Christian that makes sense and feels empowering?

Although my 30- and 40-something-year-old children raise these kinds of questions with their doting dad and devoted granddad, the church does not often hear or deal with these kinds of questions. In my day, we referred to these as "parking lot "questions. These were the kinds of concerns my generation raised after "church" was over on a Sunday afternoon, as we gave voice to our frustrations with one another while still on the church property. Today, these questions are seldom raised at church at all. They are now raised by a generation who is daring the church to be the church while firmly having at least one foot firmly planted outside even the parking lot.

This generation is calling for a reinvention of church. They want to see the church doing its thing in light of twenty-first century realities and challenges, and engaging its ministry "on purpose"— with intentionality and authenticity. Each section of this book is practical: solid scholarship and presentation followed by reflection, with a series of questions for consideration by the individual or group reading it. The volume that Bond and Cheifetz have so deftly coedited is intended for practical engagement. They are focused on addressing the concerns of and developing whole persons. In their words, "This is an adjustment, not a demolition."

I, for one, welcome their argument that adjustments, reconstructions, and reinventions are indeed called for, without our having to demolish the whole historic enterprise. The cohort of leaders who contribute to this volume have each demonstrated excellence in their own area of ministry. Readers will find reasoned and relevant perspectives that will assist all of us on our attempt to do church on purpose.

Rev. Dr. Aidsand F. Wright-Riggins III
Executive Director, American Baptist Home Mission Societies

about the CONTRIBUTORS

ADAM L. BOND, CO-EDITOR
An ordained minister in the American Baptist Churches USA, Dr. Adam L. Bond currently works as Associate Professor of Historical Studies and American Baptist liaison at the Samuel DeWitt Proctor School of Theology at Virginia Union University in Richmond. His previous ministry work included serving for six years on the American Baptist Churches of Wisconsin staff and writing for *Judson Bible Journeys for Adults*. He has an MDiv from Samuel DeWitt Proctor School of Theology, and a PhD and MA from Marquette University. He is author of *I've Been Called: Now What?* (Judson Press) and *The Imposing Preacher: Samuel DeWitt Proctor and Black Public Faith* (Fortress Press).

LAURA MARIKO CHEIFETZ, CO-EDITOR
Rev. Laura Mariko Cheifetz serves as Executive Director of Church & Public Relations at the Presbyterian Publishing Corporation. She received her MDiv from McCormick Theological Seminary and her MBA from North Park University, both in Chicago, Illinois. She is an ordained Teaching Elder in the Presbyterian Church (USA). She is a contributor to *Streams Run Uphill*, edited by Mihee Kim-Kort (Judson Press); and the author of the Afterword for *Here I Am*, edited by Grace Ji-Sun Kim (Judson Press); and the co-author of "Forming Asian Leaders for North American Churches" in *Religious Leadership: A Reference Handbook* (SAGE Publications, Inc.).

KYLE E. BROOKS
Kyle E. Brooks is a proud native of Detroit, Michigan, and a current PhD student in the Graduate Department of Religion at Vanderbilt University in Nashville, Tennessee, concentrating in Homiletics and

Liturgics. He completed his undergraduate and master's studies at Yale University. Among his varied pursuits, he is an ordained minister, an accomplished poet, and a musician. His research interests include African American literature, homiletic theory and analysis, and performance studies.

Kyle is a doctoral fellow with the Forum for Theological Education, as well as a fellow in the Program in Theology and Practice at Vanderbilt University. He has presented his work at the Southeastern Commission for the Study of Religion (SECSOR) Conference and the Academy of Homiletics. He hopes to build a career in the academic study and teaching of religion while also maintaining commitments to ministerial education and praxis in local congregations.

THERESA E. CHO

Rev. Theresa E. Cho grew up in Reno, Nevada, and graduated from McCormick Theological Seminary in Chicago, Illinois, with awards in preaching and theology. Before coming to St. John's in 2003, she completed a full-year chaplain residency program at UCSF Medical Center, where she provided spiritual care to patients, families, and staff. Rev. Cho is active in all levels of the Presbyterian Church (USA), and served as Moderator for the Presbytery of San Francisco. She has experience teaching children with special needs and working in multiracial urban congregations in Chicago and in Seoul, Korea. She has published articles and written blogs in *Christian Century*, *Presbyterian Leader*, *Sojourners'* God's Politics, Christians for Biblical Equality, ecclesio.com, and other blog sites. She can be contacted at www.theresaecho.com.

LESLIE COPELAND-TUNE

Rev. Dr. Leslie Copeland-Tune is currently Director of Communications & Resource Development for the DC Baptist Convention. She previously served as Assistant Director of Justice and Advocacy for the National Council of the Churches of Christ in the USA, where she used her gifts to add a Christian voice to women's issues, ending poverty, and other national and international concerns. She also served on the National Council of Churches's Special Commission for the Just Rebuilding of the Gulf Coast, which helped to advocate for the people of the Gulf Coast following the massive devastation of Hurricanes Katrina and Rita. Rev. Dr. Copeland-Tune was ordained to the gospel ministry in 2001, under the leadership of Rev. Dr. H. Beecher Hicks Jr. at Metropolitan Baptist Church in Washington, DC. Until 2008, Dr. Copeland-Tune served as Assistant Pastor at Norbeck Community Church in Silver Spring, Maryland.

JONATHAN A. MALONE

Rev. Dr. Jonathan A. Malone grew up in Albany, New York, where he attended Emmanuel Baptist Church. He went to Oberlin Conservatory of Music for two years and then transferred to the Crane School of Music at the State University of New York, Potsdam, graduating with a Bachelors of Music. He received his MDiv from Andover Newton Theological School and his PhD in Theology from the University of Dayton. His dissertation was on Baptist Ordination. Dr. Malone has served churches in Ohio, Pennsylvania, and since 2009, in East Greenwich, Rhode Island. Author of the blog *Theological Snob* and host of the podcast *Twelve Enough* (both can be found at www.twelveenough.com), Dr. Malone has also been published in *The Journal of Ecumenical Studies* and *The American Baptist Quarterly*.

MADELINE McCLENNEY-SADLER

A native of Richmond, Virginia, Rev. Dr. Madeline McClenney-Sadler accepted a call to ministry in high school. In 1989 she was licensed to preach, and in 1993 she was ordained to ministry to the homeless by New Bethel Baptist Church in the District of Columbia. Dr. McClenney-Sadler holds a Bachelor of Business Administration in Finance and an MDiv from Howard University in Washington, DC. At Duke University she earned a PhD in Old Testament Studies, with minors in Women's Studies and Islamic Law. In 1999, while completing the dissertation, she founded Exodus Foundation.org, a Christian faith-based charity dedicated to serving formerly incarcerated African Americans and those at risk for incarceration. Dr. McClenney-Sadler is author of *Recovering the Daughter's Nakedness: A Formal Analysis of Israelite Kinship Terminology and the Internal Logic of Leviticus 18* (her doctoral dissertation), and contributor to *Mother Goose, Mother Jones, Mommie Dearest: Biblical Mothers and Their Children*, edited by Cheryl Kirk-Duggan and Tina Pippin (Society of Biblical Literature) and *Ministry with Prisoners and Families: The Way Forward*, edited by W. Wilson Goode Sr., Charles E. Lewis Jr., and Harold Dean Trulear (Judson Press).

JESSICA VAZQUEZ TORRES

Jessica has 15 years of experience in antiracism, anti-oppression, and cultural competency workshop development and facilitation. She is active in peace and justice concerns, including worker justice, immigration reform, and antiracism. She is deeply committed to addressing social structures and cultural dynamics that marginalize and minoritize communities and limit their access to resources. A 1.5-generation ESL queer Latina of Puerto Rican descent, Jessica holds a bachelor's degree in Criminal Justice from the University of Central Florida, an MDiv from Christian Theological Seminary, and a Master of Theological Studies from the Candler School of Theology at Emory University. She is a member of the Presbyterian Church (USA), and was previously an ordained minister in the Christian Church (Disciples of Christ).

JAMIE P. WASHAM

Rev. Jamie P. Washam has served as pastor of Underwood Memorial Baptist Church in Wauwatosa, Wisconsin, since the fall of 2003. The church is a diverse body of believers, committed to social justice and God's radically inclusive love. A native Texan, Rev. Washam earned a BA in History from the University of Texas at Austin and an MDiv at the Harvard Divinity School. She makes her home with her beloved husband and sweet son in Milwaukee, Wisconsin. As an agent of God's love in the universe, she considers it an honor to get paid to do what she would do in her free time anyway.

REV. REGINALD W. WILLIAMS JR.

Rev. Reginald W. Williams Jr. serves proudly as Pastor of First Baptist Church of University Park. Previously, he served as Associate Pastor for Justice Ministries at the Trinity United Church of Christ where he was ordained under Rev. Dr. Jeremiah A. Wright Jr. A native of Chicago, Rev. Williams holds a BS in Business Administration from Florida A&M University, a Juris Doctor from the University of Wisconsin, and an MDiv from the Samuel DeWitt Proctor School of Theology at Virginia Union, where he is currently working toward his DMin. With Danielle Ayers, Williams is coauthor of *To Serve This Present Age: Social Justice Ministry in the Black Church* (Judson Press).

preface

SOME OF THE BEST CONVERSATIONS THAT WE HAVE HAD ABOUT church have rarely happened within the places where our congregations meet. Do not get us wrong; the church is a wonderful place. The church has nurtured us and created space for us to explore our sense of vocational purpose. Church is a great community—for many things. There is the music, and the food, and the inspiration, and the people. A lot of great things happen within the life of the church. In many instances, however, the church has not been the best incubator for new ideas and/or traditions. So, yes, some of the best conversations that we have had about church often happen outside the places where our congregations meet.

We decided to place our musings in print. Adam thought about all of the "meetings after the meeting" talks that he had with colleagues. Those talks led him to think about the ways in which thirty- and forty-somethings could "reinvent" church. Many of us budding church leaders are finding our way into leadership positions in local churches and denominational settings. In some spaces, we are invited to share what is really on our minds. In other spaces we are, well . . . not so much. Our challenge, then, has been to find ways to integrate ourselves into the march to Zion that is the tradition of our respective church traditions. Our sources on the ground suggest that we could be doing some different things in our various congregations and religious settings. The gospel and need for the church is relevant. But some of our practices are dated.

We write this text knowing that someone may write the same thing about us in thirty years. We realize that older and younger generations will interrogate our perspectives. We will be challenged on the basis of our idealism or lack of "radicality." Or, this text may be too conservative for generations in the years to come. We accept that. But we are concerned about what is going to happen to the mainline churches. We do not want the church and its ministry to teeter on the fence of relevance. We also want the text to give readers of any generation hope. In these pages you will find the words and passions of a committed group of ministry leaders who care about the church. *Church on Purpose* is not an attempt to break from or reject tradition. We love—most of—the practices and experiences that nurtured us. At the same time, we are intent upon thinking and praying with the church about its future.

The book has three parts. Each part has implicit questions that guide its content. The first part offers opportunities to think deeply about being a disciple. How does one learn, worship, witness, lead, and/or preach? This question guides the writers in their diverse approaches to the issues within their ministry contexts. Part two invites the reader to dream about a new way of being church. How can we embrace and adapt to the changes that take place in our congregations and denominations? The final part encourages the reader to live in ways that combat alienation. The authors of these essays challenge us to think about the age-old question: Who is my neighbor?

Laura and I are grateful for each other and for the contributors who agreed to share their "big idea" with you in print. I approached Laura after sitting on this book idea for a couple of years. She willingly agreed to join the cause and to recruit some people with something meaningful to say. Some authors came to this project later than others, so their deadline snuck up on them right away. (Sorry about that!) Thank you for agreeing to work under that pressure.

We are grateful to Rebecca Irwin-Diehl and the Judson Press staff for their work on our behalf. This committed group of people cares about its authors and audience. They are invested in having and hosting the conversation. And for this, we are grateful.

Thank you for taking time to purchase and read this book. We hope that you are able to find common ground with us. Or, you may find in this text a spark that ignites your own plans for reinventing church. Regardless of where and why you enter, may this book be an opportunity for you to reflect upon the meaning of our journey as a called-out community of believers.

Adam L. Bond
Laura Mariko Cheifetz

Part I

Reinventing Discipleship

1

POLITICS, MONEY, SEX, and MORE

Faith Formation in Today's Church

ADAM L. BOND

"Life application" has become a popular catchphrase amongst churchgoers and casual Christians. Many persons use this phrase as a factor in determining the credibility and relevance of the preacher-pastor and her or his ministry of preaching. The preacher-pastor who can make the Scripture apply to life is an attractive candidate for our attention span on Sunday mornings. Televangelists and radio preachers gain some following due to their "life application" sermons. I would have money enough for a meal (well, at least $27.00) if I received a dollar from every person who has praised the "life application" preaching of a prominent radio or television preacher. There is even the popular *Life Application Study Bible*,[1] which touts its ability to apply the Scripture to life's circumstances. That is the goal for any good preacher and teacher in the church. To be sure, we want the person in the pew and the classroom to find relevance in the Bible that we preach and teach. But what if I told you that some of us churchgoers look for application that we cannot find in many congregational settings? Would you be surprised or upset to hear that some congregations avoid or neglect some of the major themes and issues of the Bible? And in this act of avoidance—or neglect—they lack the kind of allure that draws some young and middle-aged adults to congregational formation events beyond the Sunday morning worship.

The Sunday church school is one of the long-standing practices of many Protestant congregations. On a given Sunday a person can show up at, say, a Baptist, Methodist, or Pentecostal congregation at roughly 9:00 a.m. and find people reading educational literature for the faithful Christian. You can sit in a variety of Christian education classes across the country and hear a central focus emerge from the sharing of participants: piety. To be sure, Sunday school lesson writers are inclined to nurture the piety of the Christian believer. They seek to answer several implied questions (e.g., How might I be saved? How do I pray more effectively? Will God answer my prayers? Am I a good Christian?). Or, the writers reinforce notions and concepts that most Christians already believe (e.g., Jesus is the answer to all of life's circumstances. God hears our prayers and answers them.). The teachers and students who receive the curriculum view the Scripture through similar questions and statements. But people need an informed faith perspective for every aspect of life. I want to reinvent the Christian education ministry by arguing for a new way to write and interpret the curriculum. This essay will present four critical emphases for the future of Christian education in numerous congregations. The result, I believe, should be lessons and sermons that focus on improving the political, ecological, financial, and sexuality literacies of their readers and hearers.

The Average Baptist Church, Everywhere, USA

Please allow me to channel my wife's favorite television show of all time, *The Golden Girls*. Picture it: Everywhere, USA, 1990s.

A young man in his early twenties walks into the Sunday church school class and sits in the adult class #1. He is the youngest person in the room by twenty years. He is excited about participating in the class and feels a sense of pride at being a part of the *adult* class. His questions are new and foreign to him. He has voted in one election, and another is on the horizon. The class begins with prayer and moves quickly into reading the Scripture. After a few passages, the instructor asks the first reader to interpret the meaning of the verses. Another reader follows the first. The instructor asks, stopping the reader after two verses, "What do those verses mean?" After the third reader, the young man noticed two trends. First, the instructor had the participants teaching the class (which is not a bad teaching practice, if used properly). Second, the participants had some form of the same response: "This was what God/Jesus desired to happen." Or, "This prepared the way for Jesus." The instructor concluded the lesson by encouraging the class to read next week's lesson and dedicate time in prayer. Sound familiar?

Anxious to become more involved in his growth and spiritual formation, the young man mentioned in this story attended the church's Bible study. He listened closely as the instructor invited persons to read the Scripture for the session. The instructor transitioned into a lecture about becoming more like Jesus "in our walk and in our talk." The young man sat and wondered how to insert his questions about God and the upcoming election into the conversation. At no point did the young man sense a concern about how to navigate the big issues of life (i.e., politics, global warming, etc.). From what he could hear, persons were more concerned about how to avoid becoming ineligible for heaven. Something about this did not seem right. But he did not give it much thought.

The young man figured out a few things that day. The conversations he heard were similar to the church school classes that he attended as a child. He did, however, pause and question what he was hearing: Is Christianity just about who gets to go to heaven? Is the goal of our Christian beliefs and practices similar to the directions that we receive on an airplane? (Secure your oxygen mask—that is, your spot in paradise—before attempting to help the person next to you.) These questions haunted me—I mean, the young man—for several years. My answers led me to the conclusion that I previewed earlier in this text. We can make room in our education ministries for four major curriculum topics: politics, financial management, ecological stewardship, and sexuality awareness. Becoming more faith conscious and literate in these areas of everyday life is an opportunity for speaking to and with our communities of faith, especially the young adult populations.

We can reinvent Christian education to attend to more than the otherworldly hopes that our faith embraces. An adjustment to the way that we interpret biblical texts, and their shaping influence on our faith, can steer us into a model of teaching and learning that addresses the concerns of the whole person. This is an adjustment, not a demolition. We have much within our Christian traditions and practices upon which we can build. Consider, then, the opportunities and reasons that exist for addressing those "seedy" topics of politics, money, pollution, and sex. Within our Bible is material enough to think critically and deeply about the meaning of our faith in these areas. Avoiding them, then, might suggest that we are either too immature to deal with them or feel ill-equipped to address them in a classroom setting. But there may be no better place for persons of faith to have these conversations. To be sure, people do not come to church to memorize the names of the tribes of Israel. God has something to say to us about all areas of our lives. Reinventing our Christian education content and delivery is an important step to provide clarity in sharing such important material for faith formation. We, the body of believers, have a call and obligation to discern God's messages for the whole person—for the living of *these* days.

The Bible and Politics

The Bible is replete with stories and ideas that deal with politics. It covers, almost religiously, the role of politics in the lives of its religious traditions—Judaism and Christianity. Political literacy, therefore, should be a goal for the Christian. We are not just citizens of the kingdom of God. We Christians are citizens of states and countries that have laws that govern our lives. We can say the same about the persons who lived in our sacred texts. Moses, Deborah, Saul, David, Amos, Joseph and Mary, Jesus, Paul, and others—all of them present us with stories that show the intersection of the religious and the political. What shall we do with such interesting and compelling narratives of faith? One cannot read very far through the biblical texts without confronting questions of governance. God gave to humankind "dominion" over the earth. (I will say more about this text in our section on ecological literacy.) What does our authority mean, and what systems or ways of organizing ourselves help us to express it? The use of this authority has been and remains a constant struggle in our world. How might our biblical sources reveal ways of engaging God's presence and wisdom for our journeys as citizens of the world? I invite you to consider the witness of three biblical texts: Exodus 3–4, Judges 4–5, and Matthew

22:15-22. These Scriptures present sample texts for lessons that invite readers to think theologically and politically. In other words, the Bible gives us permission to talk about God and politics.

Moses and Pharaoh

The account of Israel's exodus from Egypt is a familiar tale for the Sunday church school student. The story has been so compelling throughout time that persons have invoked the power of the narrative during various social circumstances in history. In 1998 a popular animated movie based upon the story, *The Prince of Egypt*, borrowed from this lore. The children of Israel are bondservants to the Egyptians. They long for relief but see no way to get it. Moses, minding his own business on Mount Horeb, receives instructions from God through a burning bush to give the king of Egypt a message: "Let my people go." Pharaoh refused to release the Hebrew people from captivity. But Moses reluctantly embraced the prophetic mantle. He spoke truth to power and assisted in securing freedom for his people.

Although the story is familiar, the way we tell it can know nuance and innovation. Many of us as teachers and leaders within Christian education settings are quick to celebrate the narrative's moment of freedom from bondage. We highlight Pharaoh's defeat in the Red Sea as divine retribution, and we tout the power of God throughout the process. These are wonderful things to celebrate. An emphasis on these things, however, can divert our attention from other matters. For example, there is a real conversation to be had from this text about immigration. In Exodus 3:7-12 God assures Moses of having heard the Israelites' cry. God promises to deliver them from Egypt into a land flowing with milk and honey. That land, however, already has residents: the Canaanites, Hittites, Amorites, Perizzites, Hivites, and Jebusites. But God tells the Israelites that this will be their land. As students and instructors, we can see how this text presents opportunities for dialogue and challenges to inherited notions about this story. The things that the Israelites do to possess the land, moreover, are also important matters for conversation. So I celebrate what this might mean for the relevance of our time of study and reflection. We will have a lesson that speaks to more than our personal piety. We will engage other serious matters that push us to think about the meaning of our faith.

Before continuing with the other texts, I must establish a few ideas. First, politics can be a civil topic of public conversation. (Our current environment may suggest otherwise.) As persons of faith, we do not do each other harm by disagreeing. In Baptist contexts, in fact, we would worry if we all agreed about everything. Second, the Christian community can welcome the opportunity to explore what God might have to say about our existence as political citizens. If the responsible act of citizenship is to vote, we should understand the principles of faith that inform our political decisions. Where is the safe space to develop those principles of faith? The church! We have opportunities within our church calendar to think deeply about something more than a passing word from the pulpit during election season. Third, did I mention that the Bible deals with politics in at least sixty-five of the sixty-six books?

Deborah and Barak

If the following passage does not beg for a conversation about faith and politics, I do not know what does:

> [1]The Israelites again did what was evil in the sight of the LORD, after Ehud died. [2]*So the* LORD *sold them into the hand of King Jabin of Canaan,* who reigned in Hazor; the commander of his army was Sisera, who lived in Harosheth-ha-goiim.[3] Then the Israelites cried out to the LORD for help; for he had nine hundred chariots of iron, and had oppressed the Israelites cruelly twenty years. [4]At that time Deborah, a prophetess, wife of Lappidoth, was judging Israel. (Judges 4:1-4 NRSV [italics added])

Without offering the context for this passage, we probably can find several different things to highlight for conversation. The Israelites did evil in the sight of the Lord. God sold them to the king of Canaan. The Israelites asked God for help because the king of Canaan oppressed them for years, probably with the aid of his strong military support. There was a prophetess, Deborah, who held the Israelites accountable for their social and ethical life. These are important details and rich information from which we can have several conversations. From God's hand in political affairs to women in leadership both political and religious, the Bible provides lessons for the thoughtful Christian.

An angle to this story moves the conversation beyond politics proper. Deborah works with a young leader, Barak. She instructs him with military strategy and enlists his help in bringing it to pass. He would take ten thousand warriors with him and secure a victory for his people by following her directions. They win, and the people celebrate. This story has the type of depth that can hold our attention. Consider the following lesson objectives for a Sunday school class. By the end of this lesson the participant will

1. develop a position on religion and violence;
2. compare possible justifications for war in the text to notions about war among religious people in our time;
3. create a chart that identifies various "Christian" reasons for/against enacting a military campaign.

Imagine what we could explore and discover in a session guided by these objectives. Such a conversation is almost always timely in a post-9/11 world. The Arab Spring, more recent events in Syria, and continued counterterrorism issues invite dialogue from concerned Christians. If the president of the United States takes certain matters to Congress, what will be the voice of the people in our legislators' ears? What do we believe God has to say—to us, to the world—about these important matters?

Jesus Said, "Give to Caesar . . . ," and Paul Said, "Pray for Him"

The story about tax collection in Matthew 22:15-22 is an engaging one to consider for this essay. Imagine the debates that would take place if we told politically diverse Christians to develop a faith statement on taxes using this text. Consider the context of the statement "Give to Caesar what is his." The Pharisees ask Jesus if their religion and way of life deemed it lawful to pay taxes. Can't you hear them? "Jesus, since you know so much about what God thinks, tell us, is it right to pay taxes?" This question and Jesus' response offer important ways to engage such questions. Ask them! Regardless of the Pharisees' intent, somebody wants to know the answer. As persons of faith, what is our responsibility to society? What does God expect of us as citizens? That is the fundamental question. To be sure, we all can agree on most of what Paul said in 1 Timothy 2:1-4. Pray for people in high office. Check. I did that this morning while watching the news. But our responsibility does not end with prayer.

We cannot deny the prophetic witness of the eighth-century BCE prophets. "Let justice roll down like waters," Amos proclaimed (Amos 5:24). Amos's conversation with God suggested that God was not pleased with religious activities. Justice matters to God. Citizenship does not mean an outright acceptance of "democratic" politics. If one accepts the state of democracy as is, one resigns oneself to the issues that plague the world. But that notion, I believe, is not the faith that we proclaim. God requires more than taxes and a trip to the voting booth every two or four years.

Beyond the Bible: Christians and the State

Christians have struggled for centuries with their relationship with the empire/state. Before joining with the imperial leader Constantine in the early fourth century, Christians faced the "Great Persecution" under the Roman emperor Diocletian. The relationship between church and state would change again and again over time. Puritans left for the "New Land" due to their relationship with England's monarchs. The Puritan vision for the colonies produced a God-conscious culture. The citizens of the emerging American republic sought to produce checks and balances that would keep any specific religious group from dictating the direction of the nation. As the new residents sought independence, enslaved African and African American Christians spoke out about slavery. This was a social-religious issue. It was not one or the other. Freedom from sin and slavery was God's will for humankind, they proclaimed. These are not the only major issues in Christian history. Some are closer to our time.

Consider the following examples of conversations between faith and citizenship. Skepticism over the allegiance of a Roman Catholic candidate for president almost kept John F. Kennedy out of the highest office in the land. Whom would Kennedy serve? Would he serve the pope? Or was he "American enough" to know his primary allegiance? Many of us are aware of the impact of the Moral Majority. Jerry Falwell was an influential Baptist preacher whose legacy and voice shaped political conversations especially in the late 1970s through the 1990s. His voice was a reaction to the prophetic witness of the Civil Rights Movement and the social-religious influence of preachers and lay leaders in the struggle for justice in America. From "faith-based initiatives" to the controversial sermons of Jeremiah Wright, pious catchphrases, sound bites, and slogans attempt to connect religion and politics in American life. Religion, with Christianity as a notable expression of it in the United States, continues to inform and shape the nature of debates for civil society.

Political literacy is a must for Christians. Developing a true Christian conscience on such matters requires time spent in discernment. We need our religious education to help us sift through the messages that society feeds into every possible communication outlet. Our local services (schools, libraries, police, fire, and sanitation departments, etc.) depend upon our participation in society. How, then, shall we vote? How does our faith inform that vote? What does it mean to be a citizen of God's kingdom and a citizen of this country, of the world? These questions are too relevant and pressing to avoid them in our churches. As church, we teeter on the verge of irrelevance when we refuse to offer responsible "God talk" that interrogates our responsibilities as residents of this world.

The Bible and the Environment

Ecological or environmental literacy deserves a spot in our reinvented curriculum. Take a moment to complete the following exercise. Define these terms: "pollution," "environmental racism," "going green," "recycling," "conservation."

Scripture tells us about God's relationship with the environment. "The earth is the Lord's and all that is in it, the world, and those who live in it; for he has founded it on the seas, and established it on the rivers" (Psalm 24:1-2 NRSV). God feeds the birds and clothes the grass with lilies. The biblical text also specifies humankind's relationship with the environment. "God said, 'See, I have given you every plant yielding seed that is upon the face of all the earth, and every tree with seed in its fruit; you shall have them for food'" (Gen. 1:29

NRSV). We are interdependent. We need the plants and the animals as much as these things need us. What do these messages say about God and God's creation? How do we translate them for today? Yes, Scripture also tells us that humankind's relationship with creation is one of authority. But authority does not mean exploitation. When and how might we cross the line? These are important matters to consider. The Bible invites us to develop beliefs about our place in creation. Using the Christian education curriculum for this purpose, then, is a good investment of our time and faith.

Authority versus Exploitation

Concern for the earth and its creation is an act of stewardship. We (should) care for what God has given us. Moreover, people, plants, and animals share space and resources. Violating the terms of this relationship creates an imbalance. What if we were to reinterpret the Genesis account? In Genesis 2 God gave purpose to creation. Maybe one of the problems in the garden was the exploitation of something for which God had not designed it. Someone and some things are affected when that takes place. The story states that God did not design the tree of knowledge for food. The use of its fruit, although it was edible, compromised the integrity of the environment. Determining responsible ethics for appreciating creation is an important Christian duty that requires awareness of and sensitivity to God's desire for the ecology of Earth.

Environmental Health and the Health of Creation

National Food Desert Awareness Month rolls by with little fanfare each September. It is another "awareness" category among the many on our calendars. It started as a project of the National Center for Public Research. The goal of this project is to educate people about the lack of heart-healthy foods and produce in numerous neighborhoods across the United States. In some neighborhoods convenience stores, which have limited food items and high prices, are the closest locations for groceries. This can create a lack of options for a healthy diet. Most people do not want to travel great distances to shop for food. Couple the limited transportation options of some lower-income families with environmentally challenging resources, and the results can be poor dietary habits. Our catalog of sermons and Christian education lessons may not account for such problems in society. As a recent awareness month (since about 2007), National Food Desert Awareness Month is not a part of many of our annual observances. Not yet as popular as the issues associated with Earth Day, the issue of food insecurity and its expression in food deserts are important.

The lack of access to fresh produce, meats, and dairy items limits people's dietary options. A meal of chips, sodas, and candy is not ideal. The saturation of fast-food restaurants in certain (urban) areas makes inexpensive food available. But these dining alternatives do not present the healthiest options. Quick-cook meals may not be ideal, either. The link, then, between health issues such as high blood pressure and diabetes and the accessibility of healthy foods may be obvious. But the indirect concern that we should connect to such an issue is an environmental one. What message do we (as a nation, state, or community) send to persons who live in places where there is a scarcity of resources? To be sure, one may not see the connection between food deserts and impoverished neighborhoods and communities. We can talk about a whole other set of concerns, however, when these issues converge. What are some of the direct correlations between environmental issues and human health? How should we struggle with addressing these issues? What is our investment in raising awareness about these issues by way of responsible God talk?

One resource for consulting the Scriptures may be the *Green Bible*.[2] I am not a spokesperson for this text, but it can assist students of the Bible with texts about "green" topics. Many of us are familiar with the red lettering of Jesus' words in the King James Version of the Bible. The *Green Bible* presents Scriptures in green that speak about creation and God's care for it. Imagine such a resource as a lectionary for ecological awareness. Not only preachers, but also the leaders of any ministry, can inform their faith in dialogue with sacred texts.

I am lobbying for more than a church "Earth Week." Telling people about the importance of turning off lights or conserving water is important and necessary. We have a responsibility to do this. Educating people about food deserts and environmental racism is important too. Woodsy Owl, the animated mascot of the U.S.

Forest Service featured in its public service announcements,[3] can have a comparable character in our children's lessons. That mascot can be a good teaching tool. And adults can address the complex environmental matters that challenge their religious worldviews.

The Bible and Money

The only times when many of us hear about money in the church is when someone asks us to give it to the church. Don't believe me? Consider the number of times that money comes up in your local congregation. Are 99 percent of those instances related to giving to the local congregation (for whatever purpose)? How many times do you hear about money as the benefit of faithful living? For some persons, these are the most common theological platforms for talking about money in the church. Some local churches may bring in consultants and/or use materials that talk about responsible financial living and biblical giving. These churches, however, are not as common as some may think. Regardless of your theological outlook (i.e., from the "prosperity gospel" to Occupy Wall Street), you can find your way into an emphasis on financial literacy.

Churches can develop financial literacy programs within the current Christian education curriculum or through extended programming. In many congregations, the only times in which church leaders talk about money are during the offering period in worship, at business meetings, and perhaps while in the midst of an annual stewardship drive. A financial literacy program can address this. Lessons will include items that help members of the church (and the community) become better managers of their resources. Such an education can highlight biblical texts that address theological concerns about finances. Budgeting, investing, philanthropy, and savings will all find their way into the literature and teachings. Financial professionals within the congregation can assist with monthly workshops on other important topics such as home ownership. Churches will then produce much more financially literate church members. In addition to these ideas, lots of good resources can supplement teachings on finances. Consider an accessible book study such as Shayna Lear's *Money on Purpose: Finding a Faith-filled Balance* (Judson Press) or a magazine such as *Black Enterprise* and its "wealth for life principles."[4] Michelle Singletary's "Color of Money" column in the *Washington Post* and her books provide needed commentary on important financial matters. She is also a person of faith who does not disconnect her beliefs from her understanding of money. You may be aware of other resources. While writing this essay, I received an e-mail about the Criterion Institute's initiative on the church as an economic being.[5] I am always amazed at the growing number of organizations that dedicate resources to these matters.

American Christianity as Capitalist Christianity?

The church is shaped and influenced by several contextual factors (i.e., cultures, traditions, and beliefs). Capitalism is a dialogue partner for American Christianity. The "market" is a part of our language and our actions. But the church may need to be aware of how much of a stake it has invested in the capitalist system. Adam Smith's philosophy probably has less in common with Jesus' idea about rich people than we may want to believe. So I ask you, how has our financial culture(s) shaped our ideas about money? I do not have an answer. But the question is a step toward naming those things that complement or contradict our theology of money. Imagine what a Jubilee Year (Leviticus 25) would have looked like before the housing crisis of the early 2000s. Space here is short, so I will suggest a few topics for a curriculum resource or Bible study:

- vocational development for career exploration
- homeownership
- retirement and estate planning
- investments
- tithing
- debt management and reduction
- budgeting
- credit cards and credit scores
- job interview skills

Money Matters

Money as a resource for life matters on many levels. But is it the end of a certain Christian expression or the means of it? In other words, does money define my faithfulness—giving or receiving?

Or, is money an aspect of my Christian faith that demonstrates the way(s) in which I support God's ministry on Earth? Either way, it should not be the basis for using 1 Timothy 6:10, "The love of money is a root of all kinds of evil, and in their eagerness to be rich some have wandered away from the faith and pierced themselves with many pains" (NRSV), to make the person in the pew feel guilty. For it is irresponsible to throw that verse or Malachi 3:8, "Will anyone rob God? Yet you are robbing me! But you say, 'How are we robbing you?' In your tithes and offerings!" (NRSV), as a dagger without providing critical financial literacy instruction. Everyone in the church probably would be amazed by the amount of "good" or bad debt that people carry. Teaching people sensible, accessible ways to manage all of their resources while building their ethic of stewardship may help our congregations thrive.

The Bible and Sexuality

I often joke with my students in the seminary, "There are really only sixty-five books in the Bible." They look at me like I'm crazy and worry about my salvation. Finally, some brave soul asks me why I would say such a thing. I proceed to share with the class that Song of Solomon is one of the most ignored books in the Bible, almost to the point that many people wish it away. Why is that? The book speaks of the love (however erotic) that two people share. There are, to be sure, very graphic descriptions of that love. But what makes this a problem for preaching content and Sunday school material? Granted, we may need to debate about the appropriate age group for this material. But the book is in the Bible. So what is the best way to incorporate the topic in general into our faith formation moments? We can start by acknowledging that most of the people listed in the Bible had sex. We can end by asking ourselves, "What is a responsible, healthy Christian ethic of sexuality?" With that in mind, we could construct the materials that inform our children's ideas about sex (we could do this for our adults too).

The Bible presents different views of sex. Sex is expressed in the biblical mandate to humankind to be fruitful and multiply (Genesis 1:28). So we know that many biblical characters participated in sexual activities that we can celebrate. Genealogy narratives show us that sex happened and that good people are the product of sex happening. The Gospel of Matthew helps us see this. The long account of Jesus' ancestors that begins the book (Matthew 1:1-17) gives us the context for his arrival. We should not forget the sensual content of Song of Solomon. The pleasure associated with sex in that book is obvious. Like many other things, however, sex has the potential to disrupt human-divine relationships.

Sex, No Sex, Same Sex

I would guess that most readers of this essay are aware of the sex-abuse scandal in the Roman Catholic Church. In 2002 the public learned of the problems in the Archdiocese of Boston. There were reports that several priests in Boston sexually abused hundreds of children over a period of decades.[6] The attention given to that matter unveiled countless accounts of similar incidents across the nation. These cases raised questions about issues of sex, of homosexuality (as all of the priests were men and many of the victims were boys), and of clerical celibacy. As a graduate student in a Jesuit university, I could not avoid conversations about the matter. But it was one of the few times in my life, outside of seminary, that I heard church people talk about sex in a constructive manner. Sure, the tone of the conversations was not always civil. Yet, church people were saying more than "people shouldn't fornicate." This led me to one conclusion: we cannot talk about sex responsibly until we are able to talk openly about sex as a God-given gift.

Body versus Spirit in Christian Thought

Modern Christianity inherited an idea that we should consider in this conversation. The idea splits the human being into two: body and soul. If one is out of whack, the other will follow. The body has been the traditional frontline of the battleground against evil. If a person can get her or his body in check, the soul will be okay—and vice versa. That is why conversations about original sin are so instructive. History has given us persons who have argued that the original sin of Adam and Eve in the garden of Eden was sexual in nature. Their eyes, some say, lusted for what was wrong to have. Christians throughout time have had a hard time dealing with sex and sexuality. In America race and religion have sometimes meshed to muddy the waters of healthy talk about sexuality. For example, in the nineteenth century some justifications for slavery were based upon caricatures of black people and their bodies. Black men were cast as beasts who lacked civil instincts and etiquette. They were seen as hypersexual monsters, and some images and writings cast black women as Jezebels. At the same time, some touted the religious fervor of enslaved persons and their naturally religious spirits. How could both ideas exist at the same time? These notions were consistent with the split.

Our biblical texts give us some of what we encounter in our body-spirit split. People look at Paul's writings (especially Romans and Galatians) and see the language: flesh and spirit. The two are at war in our minds, so we believe. Tertullian of Carthage, a celebrated author of the early church, writes a third-century letter to admonish Christian women on their attire.[7] His concern is born out of the body-spirit divide. Women should dress modestly, he said. (He paid little attention to correcting or instructing men.) But what did that do for shaping notions of modesty and sexuality for women and men? This was an authority in the church! Body image and our associations of sex with appearance and apparel matter to us. Certain body dimensions and figures are impressed upon us as being more sexually attractive than others. Images appear on television and movie screens that define what a sexually attractive person wears, what car such a person drives, and how she or he smells. How should we embrace or contest these ideas based upon our beliefs? Examining what these notions mean for our congregants may be the beginning of a healthy Christian view of sexuality.

Procreation or Pleasure

The debate will continue in some settings over the purpose of sexuality. We continue the dualism of the body-spirit conversation, however, by saying that sex is an either/or activity. Some persons suggest that the sole function and purpose of sex is procreation. Others argue that sex is an activity that God wants us to enjoy, whether or not it leads to the conception of children. (That is surely why God allowed the innovation of contraceptives!)

Because sex happens, persons sometimes take one of two theological positions. One position is that sex should happen only within the confines of a marital relationship. God blesses that sex.

The suggestion is that abstinence is the posture that one should assume if one is not married. Another position is that persons will have sex, so they should be responsible in whatever way that is. Responsibility, for these persons, may mean that sexually active adults will use contraceptives and care for and about their partner's emotional health. See the case studies below to interpret the matter for yourself. What is an appropriate Christian ethic of sexuality in your context or congregation?

Case 1. As you are walking through the halls of your congregation, you see two twelve-year-old children kissing, mouth to mouth, in a corner. You break up the action. The children ask you what is wrong with their behavior. They respond by saying that this is the way that their parents show their love for each other. Speaking to you as authority figure (pastor, deacon, elder, etc.), they say, "We love each other. Why can't we show our love for each other in this way?" What is a response that respects all of the parties involved (i.e., the children, the parents, the community, and a Christian sexual ethic)?

Case 2. A young unmarried couple approaches you to talk about the problems that they are having. They have lived together for four years, and marriage is not a part of this conversation or any that they want to have. You begin to realize that they are trying to tell you that they are concerned about the nature of their sexual activity. They suggest that the problem stems from her desire to experiment and his more "traditional" understanding of sex. What is the responsible way to deal with their concerns? How do we allow our theological beliefs about sexuality to inform our response?

Case 3. The pastor's son and his girlfriend are expecting a child. They are sixteen years old. They are among the rising number of unmarried youth in your city who are expecting. How do you address this situation? Why is it a problem and/or a blessing? What do you in your position as a leader in the church tell the rest of the children in the church?

Literacy as Reinvention: A Talking-Points Summary

1. We have an opportunity to retool our understanding of faith formation in the church. A primary way to do this is through our educational curriculum, broadly defined. This grows out of our concern for being literate in several aspects of life: the political, the ecological, the financial, and the sexual.

2. While biblical lessons that focus on faith principles for piety and a responsible devotional life are helpful, we realize that God has something to say specifically about these fundamental areas of our life.

3. This alternative approach will allow persons a vision of educational moments that expand our notion of faithful discipleship—discipleship education, even.

4. A primary concern of this essay is the church's continued relevance. We no longer live in the age of *Leave It to Beaver* or *The Brady Bunch*. Images on television, print, and social media show the decreasing tendency of people to label matters of sex and sexuality as taboo. Our goal, therefore, as church could be interpreting and translating the ways in which our faith can make us literate and engaged in the contemporary world. That requires Christian education materials (and teachers) that are intentional about connecting the Bible to and theological reflection that does not hide from the "real world."

5. Enhancing the educational curriculum of the church also means that we make education a priority in the church. Many of our churches promote Christian education with time slots on the schedule, but there is a waning concern for making the "education hour" a whole-life event in the congregation. We place the real focus on Sunday morning. Implicitly, Sunday morning is mandatory; all other events are extra credit. We know some of the reasons for this phenomenon: fundraising, music, and so on.

6. One should not, however, limit the notion of an educational curriculum to Sunday morning church school. Every moment in the life of the church that seeks to nurture its members is an opportunity to make people literate in the areas listed above. We have the potential to align youth ministry, vacation Bible school, new members' class, Bible study, and the sermon to the four areas of literacy. We can, moreover, place in harmony the expressed educational curriculum with the implied one. That is, we can sync what we believe we teach with what our actions and words really teach.

7. Beginning with political literacy, one can find its significance in the other areas that I addressed. Elections across the country have had on their ballots issues of sexuality, ecology, and finances. These issues are interconnected and related. We live in an ecosystem that bears the brunt of the negative impact of our choices in grooming

and cleaning products. Our history bears witness to Christianity's constant interaction with "the world." Most of us choose not to embrace the monastic life. Our choice as responsible Christians, therefore, can be to prepare persons to read and navigate the social constructs that will allow us to be faithful to the God we serve.

Questions for Consideration

1. What issues are important for you to hear in your faith development?
2. What ideas in this essay contradict your understanding of the Christian's responsibility?
3. What kind of immediate changes can your church make to be more intentional about educating the congregation on these faith matters?

Notes

1. *Life Application Study Bible* (Wheaton, IL: Tyndale House, 1991).

2. *The Green Bible* (San Francisco: HarperOne, 2008).

3. For a good flashback video of Woodsy Owl, see http://www.youtube.com/watch?v=gZB7gSQRIuM.

4. See, at the *Black Enterprise* website, http://www.blackenterprise.com/tag/wealth-for-life-principles.

5. See, at the Criterion Institute website, http://criterioninstitute.org/1kchurches/ceb/.

6. For a rough timeline of this matter, see the *Minneapolis Star Tribune*'s coverage at http://www.startribune.com/nation/226537021.html. See also, at PBS's "Religion and Ethics Newsweekly," http://www.pbs.org/wnet/religionandethics/2002/04/05/april-5-2002-gay-priests/18385/.

7. See Tertullian of Carthage, "On the Apparel of Women," http://www.tertullian.org/anf/anf04/anf04-06.htm.

2

ENGAGING in the EVERYDAY

A Different Approach to Evangelism

JONATHAN A. MALONE

We are facing the end of Christianity as we know it. Well, maybe it is not the end, but in an American context churches are not in the same place as they were fifty years ago. No longer will people go to church out of a sense of social obligation. Sunday mornings are now times when people can sleep in, spend time with family, work on Sunday's crossword puzzle, or do other idyllic, relaxing things that do not involve sitting on a wooden bench listening to someone rant for a certain amount of time, singing arcane songs, and paying for the experience with some kind of offering. The religious landscape in America is drastically changing.

Many "church experts" have been wearing their "The End Is Near!" sandwich boards, parading around in the religious marketplace pointing out various trends such as the rise of the "nones" (those who do not affiliate with any religious tradition) and the rise of the "dones" (those who identify as Christian, but are done with institutional religion), the diminishing sizes of churches, and the decreased amount of professional respect given to the clergy as portents of the beginning of the end of Christianity in America.[1] In response, different churches and religious communities have tried to counter such trends. Some try an overt evangelism popularly seen as the often-maligned Bible thumper standing on a street corner and calling people to repent or burn. Such an approach seems to gain little traction. Others have tried to have a more capitalistic, door-buster approach, promising gifts, books, food, carwash coupons, and other trinkets so as to attract people to visit their church and then, hopefully, return the following week. Still others do what they can to attract and draw people back again and again by offering catchy, cutting-edge fonts and marketing campaigns (e.g., "This isn't your parents' church") coupled with the most exciting, loud, high-energy service that they can offer, complete with pyrotechnics and high-flying acrobatics. While some of these approaches may work, they rest on a basic assumption about the presence of the church in the world. The assumption is that people have an under-standing of the gospel and want to go to church, and that they just need to find the right church and then they will go.

The fundamental assumption shared by the door-buster and showstopper churches is that as long as the doors are open, people will come. This approach rests on the notion that people must be lured and tempted to leave secular culture for one or two hours a week, walk through those mysterious doors, and become a part of a Christian community to one degree or another. Such an assumption continues with the idea that once inside the church, a person will experience Christianity and will want to come again. This assumes that people will have some kind of reason for attending church, even if it is out of basic curiosity. Yet if people in the broader com-munity do not have an interest in Christianity, or any knowledge about the gospel, then there may not be much reason to attend a church beyond the basic pangs of guilt that drive some people to attend worship on Christmas and/or Easter.

Such an assumption does not directly address the deep level of institutional malaise and mistrust toward Christianity that is a real force in American culture. Current scandals plaguing the institution of Roman Catholicism, angry rhetoric around sexual immorality from conservative and charismatic evangelicals on the national level coupled with clergy misconduct, and personal negative expe-riences contribute to an ethos of distrust toward Christianity. In addition, trends towards a cultural pluralization, democratization, and secularization have been and continue to be a strong part of the American social-religious landscape, adding to the cultural malaise toward Christianity.[2] The relational nature of the institution of the church (broadly construed) with American society has eroded, and the response of many Christian communities is to work harder to make sure that the doors are open and people are attracted to attend and return to worship.

I describe this as a problem of evangelism. Given the general skepticism toward Christianity as an institution, churches, by focusing on Sunday morning activities, are not effectively sharing the good news of Christ with the community in a compelling way. To a large degree, the lack of attendance and skepticism is understandable. When a relationship changes, one party in the relationship has to learn how to connect and communicate and interact with the other party in a different way. American society has been saying to Christianity, "You're just not the same person you were when we were younger and in love" (like in the 1950s), and in response Christianity is saying, "Just come back, and you'll see how I've changed. Listen to the different music. I can change!" Our evangelism needs to reflect the changed nature of our relationship with American society, and the tried-and-true methods of the 1950s will no longer work.

In order for Christianity to engage the world in a different way, the church needs to engage the world. What I suggest is that church communities train and commission evangelists who are deliberately present in different aspects of the community in order to share the gospel outside of the walls of the church. These evangelists are people from the congregation; this is a ministry that works best when done by the laity. Through these evangelists churches will be able to engage in a different and still authentic way with the larger culture.

Ordinary, Extraordinary, and Sacred

First, let us consider the different ways Christianity has traditionally engaged the larger culture in our American context. Christianity has been effectively present in what I describe as the "sacred" and the "extraordinary" of culture. The sacred is the time of worship; it is the time when people are leaving the mundane aspects of their lives to gain some kind of connection with God through and with a specific worshiping community. Congregations can invite people to join them, they can be open for visitors and seekers, but they cannot force people into this level of engagement. Our celebrated

American "Establishment Clause," found in the First Amendment of the Constitution, protects people from being forced into that sacred time; people are free to choose how and when to experience the sacred, or not to experience it at all.

The extraordinary is those times of crisis when all sense of normalcy is lost. Those who are struggling economically, are in need of food and housing, or are facing illness find themselves in the extraordinary of their lives and often look to some kind of connection with the sacred. These are the "foxhole" moments of life when people commonly are found praying to God for deliverance. I do not include evenings before school exams or those nail-biting moments before the end of a sports game. We often hear God's name invoked at these moments, but they are not moments of true extraordinary experiences. After all, it is only a game, and you could always repeat the tenth grade and still live.

Hospital chaplains are among those who most often encounter people in the extraordinary of life. They are the ones who see people in life-and-death situations—moments when people realize that control of life is out of their hands. In moments of national tragedy many turn to churches or religious individuals for some kind of connection with the divine. In both these aspects of life, the sacred and the extraordinary, Christianity has historically had, and continues to have, a strong presence on the American religious landscape.

This leaves the "ordinary" of life. Unlike the sacred and the extraordinary, the ordinary is the dull, mundane aspect of life when one is not normally driven to fall on one's knees and pray for God's help. The ordinary are those moments of life that are not noticed as they pass by. Brushing your teeth, driving the daily commute, getting that morning cup of coffee, and on and on—these are are the ordinary of life. We go through the ordinary without much flair at all, and this is not necessarily a bad thing. The ordinary is the largest part of our normal living, and for a large part of our American society the church is not a part of the ordinary. You may drive past a church while driving one child to piano lessons and another to soccer practice. But you may not notice that church while you are trying to obey various traffic laws, make sure your kids are doing homework in the car, and keep them from killing each other (or you from killing them). It is in this aspect of life that Christianity has no presence and where the evangelism that I am suggesting is needed most.

Ordinary Evangelism

The type and approach of evangelism that I am suggesting deliberately engages people in the ordinary of life. These evangelists are people who have jobs, who take their children to sports events, who go to bars and coffee shops. These evangelists are a part of the ordinary and in the ordinary. As I previously stated, this ministry works best when done by the laity because they are the ones who are already in the ordinary of life. The key is in the way in which the evangelist makes his or her presence known in the community. The evangelist is not being placed in a specific place, but rather is claiming the space and the place in which he or she already resides. Yet it needs to be done in a way that does not remove the sense of the ordinary from the context for the evangelist or for any other. Rather than dressing in a special shirt with a clerical collar, or wearing a pointed hat and carrying a staff, the evangelist has a way to share the Christian gospel that does not suggest that he or she is separated as a person from others (as many assume occurs with clergy). Instead, the evangelist has a deliberate but nonthreatening way to "announce" his or her presence in that community. For example, the evangelist could hand out a business card every couple of months that says something like this:

> Hello, my name is _____. In addition to being a part of this community, I am a trained and commissioned representative of the Church of the Awesome. Beyond this card, I will not push my faith or invite you to a worship service unless asked. I want you to know that I am here, and I am willing to talk about my faith, answer any questions you may have, or hear if you need any prayers that I and my community can offer on your behalf.

Or, depending on the venue, the evangelist could put up a sign saying, "I'm a Christian. I'm here to listen, not to talk." Or, "Free Prayers—written or spoken." (Full disclosure: I have that last sign attached to the cover of my laptop because I hope to engage people in the ordinary.)

This approach to intersecting with the ordinary of society is actively passive. The evangelist offers himself or herself in an obvious way that strives to be nonthreatening. This approach will draw people's attention at first and then will likely become a part of the background. The evangelist hopes, however, not to be lost or forgotten in that background. In essence, the presence of the evangelist will bring the church further into the realm of the ordinary in ways that the institutional church is not.

Becoming an Ordinary Evangelist

All Christians are called to share the gospel, and I do not want to detract from emphasizing this aspect of each person's walk with Christ. The evangelist that I am describing deliberately goes above and beyond the basics, just as the pastor goes above and beyond in other areas of discipleship and pastoral care on behalf of the church community. There is a call to this ministry that must be named and endorsed that speaks to the nature of the relationship between the evangelist and the church community.

The church will need to commission the evangelists so that they will have the sanction and endorsement of their community. Commissioning can give a level of credibility in the broader world in the sense that the evangelist is not some lone wacko trying to start his or her own cult or religion, but rather is a part of a community and articulates a relationship between the evangelist and the congregation that he or she is representing. Once endorsed by a congregation, the evangelist is empowered to share the story of Christ with the support of the endorsing faith community. This would not occur through a Charles Finney–type, soul-stirring revival, but rather as a climax after a time of discerning and training (which I will get to later in this essay). In commissioning one person, members of the community are not only celebrating that individual's ministry but also pledging to support the evangelist in times of difficulty. It is through the evangelist that the church can have a direct presence in the ordinary of the world, and it is important that the evangelist be aware of not being alone but instead having the support and backing of a community.

Yet, it is not a one-sided relationship that is created through a commissioning. Not only is the congregation agreeing to support and help the evangelist, but also the evangelist is promising to represent the congregation in a positive and authentic way. This means that the evangelist cannot (or should not) say, for example, that being a Christian means receiving bundles and bundles of money, unless that is a belief of the community. The evangelist is not just representing Christianity; he or she also follows and practices the Christian beliefs and polity that the congregation embraces. The evangelist is sharing the language, grammar, and ethos of the endorsing congregation. One hopes that the evangelist reminds people that his or her particular understanding of Christianity is not the be-all and end-all of faith. Such an approach of humility could help to strengthen the weakened relationship between Christianity and society by showing that Christians have moved beyond their petty turf wars and different movements and no longer claim to be universally right for everyone, just particularly right for some. It would be nice if the world could see that some Christians can actually play nicely with other Christians. Regardless, the evangelist is representing a particular church and is responsible to that church.

Along with the commissioning comes training. It is a basic part of discipleship to learn and grow in education, and therefore all Christians should be involved in Bible study, prayer groups, and other areas where one can grow in faith. Yet, like the pastor and the chaplain, the evangelist is responding to a call to be present and available in the community to one degree or another, and that merits a certain level of training. The evangelist may be called on to answer the pedestrian questions, such as "How many books are there in the Bible?" or "What does God look like?" or "Do all dogs actually go to heaven?" Some training will help the evangelist respond to such questions even if it is a response such as "I don't know, but I will ask." Unlike the pastor or the chaplain, the evangelist need not undergo the years of schooling and training that prepare clergy to meet someone in the extraordinary. No one is ever fully prepared to enter into the extraordinary hell of trauma and loss; pastors and chaplains have certain skill sets to work with, as well as the conviction of a call to, that level of ministry. Yet the evangelist should have a working knowledge of Scripture, history, and theology. One of the greatest challenges to Christianity is poorly thought-out theology or a religionless spirituality that takes misunderstood aspects of Christianity or other faith traditions and appropriates them to the benefit of the individual in a skewed manner. For example, many Christians say that through the Holy Spirit God is everywhere; God is immanent. Many nonreligious people will take this aspect of Christianity and claim that because God is everywhere there is no need to be a part of a religious community, let alone ever attend a church. It is a free pass to play golf on Sundays instead of attending worship. Others may say that the most important thing is to follow the "golden rule," and as long as you do that you will be fine. It is a free pass to be nice without committing to anything.

The evangelist is an apologist in the classical sense (not in the "Believe my way or I will make you feel like a worthless person damned to hell" way, but in the "Can I share where there may be problems in such an approach?" way) and must be prepared to respond to such ideas and beliefs in at least a basic and introductory way. This does not mean that the evangelist needs to learn all of the nuanced forms of debate, how to twist an argument, or rhetorical devices to convince someone of the "truth." It means that the evangelist needs to know why she or he is a Christian, the importance of spiritual formation and support that one finds in a Christian community, and other aspects of Christian faith and tradition. Most importantly, the evangelist needs to know himself or herself as a member of the human family and a part of creation. This does not mean having all of the answers, but instead having a sense of one's personal struggles, places of questions, and places of certainty.

In addition to education around the basics of Christianity should come some basic training in personal interaction. The evangelist should have a certain level of natural charisma and should like engaging with other people. One would hope that such things would come more or less naturally. But it would not hurt for the evangelist to have some preliminary training in listening, offering support, and knowing when to refer someone to an expert. The main idea for the evangelist is to be present in the ordinary of life and to live in life, but there may be times when the evangelist is the first response to someone in the extraordinary. The evangelist may be the first shoulder someone cries on, or the first person to hear the troubled news, or the only person of faith whom an individual in distress will turn to. It is important to offer some basic training in these moments around listening, responding, and knowing when to recommend a pastor or chaplain for further help and guidance.

Within the ordinary, it is important that the evangelist learn to listen often and speak little while maintaining a sense of authenticity. This might be the most difficult aspect of being an evangelist in the ordinary: being true to oneself in every aspect of one's life. The evangelist's presence is not only to provide words but also to offer a model for a Christian life. This does not mean a model of perfection. What the evangelist can do is show that at times it is okay for a Christian to get angry, to make mistakes, to curse and cuss, and then offer contrition. The evangelist is not a pastor (who also should strive for authenticity over perfection) or a chaplain, but rather an "ordinary" Christian in the "ordinary" of life. This does not mean that the evangelist should make an effort to sin and cause a ruckus, but it does mean striving to be authentic with his or her struggles and successes. The evangelist is somebody who is a constant, deliberate presence in the ordinary of life bringing the church further into the world.

Changes to the Church

It is important to remember these words from a Sunday school song: "The church is not a building, the church is not a steeple, the church is not a resting place, the church is a people." Yet the majority of interaction between Christianity and society occurs within the walls of a church; this relationship between the church and the world is institutionalized. As I have previously stated, this seems to be the primary method of evangelization: open the doors and hope that people show up. If the church is a people, then the activities of the church should not occur exclusively within the building, but also in society through people. The primary presence of the church needs to occur through the presence of the people, not through the institution. This is engagement at a grassroots, ground level similar to a recent movement that has come to be called the "Missional Church Movement."[3] Like the Missional Church Movement, the approach that I am advocating has a deliberate nature. Yet instead of simply sending people out to be good Christians and hoping that someone notices, the congregation is commissioning specific people to be a deliberate presence in the world as a part of the congregation.[4]

What such an approach could precipitate is a new understanding of what it means to be a member of a church community. Not only does it mean that you have a place where you can go every week to hear God's word proclaimed and receive sacraments (if you lean that way), or that you have a place where you will be loved, supported, and lifted up as a child of God. Being a part of a church community will also mean that you belong to a community where you can be called and supported and challenged and commissioned. Your place in the church is not simply as a participant but as a missionary, or teacher, or evangelist, or trustee, or deacon, or any other category that has been alive in many church traditions. If the church is a people, then we need to take this seriously and make the church a people in a way that honors the various callings and ministries in each person's life and is deliberate about those callings.

Ghosts of the Past

This is not a new idea, and it does not come out of left field. We have scriptural examples suggesting the approach of evangelism that I am advocating. Within Scripture there are a number of passages endorsing the notion of one being sent with a call or ministry (e.g., 1 Samuel 16:6-13; Jeremiah 1:4-10; Acts 9:1-19). What I want churches to consider is the practice of a community's endorsement. As I have already stated, it is important that a community endorses and supports the evangelist.

We see one example of this model through the ministry of Paul. We may recall how Paul was "recruited" later in the game, after the death, resurrection, and ascension of Jesus (Acts 9:1-19); he was not one of those who had the privilege of walking with Jesus. After his conversion Paul wanted to start sharing the gospel of Jesus Christ but was aware of an understandable fear and apprehension from the leaders of the Christian movement, the original disciples in Jerusalem. In Acts 9:26-30 Paul is endorsed by Barnabas before the Jerusalem leaders and is ultimately supported by the disciples as someone who would be true to the gospel. In Acts 15:22-35 we read how the elders of the nascent movement commission and send people, including Paul, to go and share the gospel. Thus Paul, who believes that he was called to be an evangelist, approaches the leadership for endorsement. The leaders offer their endorsement to Paul and others to be evangelists. Here we see two different acts, one of acceptance and one of endorsement.[5]

In his letter to the Galatians Paul reminds the leaders of the Galatian churches of his endorsement from the council. In Galatians 1:13–2:10 we read of Paul's retelling of his conversion and his experience with the Jerusalem council. Paul reminds his readers (and listeners) how he did not share the gospel with anyone until he received the endorsement of the disciples. Galatians 2:1-2, 7-9 specifically speaks of the expressed approval and endorsement of the church "pillars" James, Peter, and John for Paul's ministry to the Gentiles. Granted, immediately following that passage Paul recounts his arguments with Peter, perhaps showing how quickly churches can fall into conflict, but the endorsement is real. The endorsement and commission of the community give credibility to Paul's ministry. Through Paul's relationship with the Jerusalem leaders we find a model of the relationship that an evangelist can have with the community. This model supports the necessary and essential relational quality between the evangelist and a church community.

Making It Happen

Such an approach will vary from church to church, community to community, and individual to individual. There is not one way to engage the ordinary of society. One of the worst things that one could do is do nothing at all, under the guise of thinking, planning, and strategizing. Instead, take a chance and start with empowering people to act on this ministry. Almost every church has that individual who is naturally outgoing, who loves to share his or her faith, and who is not easily embarrassed. Do not wait for the person to be stirred, but instead invite that person to embrace this ministry. By the same token, every church has that quiet, thoughtful individual who does not want to be showy or loud about his or her faith, but who is never embarrassed to share it. Invite that person to embrace that ministry. The point is to be proactive, to invite and take a step into the unknown of God's ministry.

After finding your first evangelists, ask for the congregation's initial approval. This would not be a final endorsement of their ministry, but the congregation is stating that they will support the training process in any way they can. It also keeps everyone in the loop. Then start the training. As already stated, basics of theology,

Scripture, and history must be covered, along with listening skills and different approaches to being present in the ordinary. Finally, have a service where the ministry of the evangelists are embraced and endorsed by the community. Empower those individuals in any and every way you can.

There is a rift between churches and society, one that does not seem to be healing. The church is not a building; it is a people. By sending people into the ordinary, the everyday parts of life, churches are engaging and being present in those aspects of life not as an institution but as a people. Trusting the Holy Spirit, we can begin to mend the rift and share the good news of Christ.

Questions for Consideration

1. What is your experience of evangelism? What evangelism efforts has your church made?
2. To what extent do you model authenticity as a Christian? What about your church? What needs to change, if anything?
3. How might you and/or your church engage people in their most ordinary moments?

Notes

1. A review in *The Christian Century* surveys a number of works describing and speaking to the decline of religion (broadly construed) in America: William McKinney, "Crunching the Numbers," *The Christian Century*, April 2, 2012, 26–29.

2. Nathan Hatch describes a democratization of Christianity in the early to middle 1800s, a trend that continues today: *The Democratization of American Christianity* (New Haven: Yale University Press, 1989). In a classic work, Peter Berger describes the effects a pluralized context has on the presence of religion in modern society: *The Sacred Canopy: Elements of a Sociological Theory of Religion* (New York: Anchor Books, 1990). Robert Wuthnow also offers a good summary of the changing religious landscape in the twentieth century: *The Restructuring of American Religion: Society and Faith Since World War II* (Princeton, NJ: Princeton University Press, 1989).

3. For more on the Missional Church Movement, see Darrell L. Guder, ed. *Missional Church: A Vision for the Sending of the Church in North America* (Grand Rapids: Eerdmans, 1998).

4. I am aware that there is a difference between commissioning and ordination. The space allotted for this essay does not allow for further investigation into this difference.

5. With this example we see what is often used as a model for endorsing missionaries. I contend that it works for evangelists, the difference being that the missionary

3

THE HEART of the MATTER
Reimagining Christian Leadership

LESLIE COPELAND-TUNE

LET'S FACE IT: THE CHURCH IS MESSY, AND CHURCH LEADERSHIP IS sometimes a "hot" mess. Think about the numerous examples that let us know how much of a mess it can be. From pastors and church leaders who steal money and engage in sexually immoral behaviors, to those who flaunt overly extravagant lifestyles and participate in ill-advised programs and activities that distort church life and "pastoral" ministry, putting the words "Christian" and "leadership" together can sometimes appear to be a contradiction. It's not that we necessarily start out trying to make a mess of things, but more often than we care to admit, as Christian leaders, our best efforts at leading sometimes end in organized disaster and controlled chaos. Not to mention that sometimes we hurt those whom we aim to help and leave people wounded and running away from, not toward, the church.

Indeed, Christians who are called to lead live in a paradoxical tension of oxymoronic behaviors and beliefs that makes our leadership efforts perhaps more difficult than it is for others. We are called out and set apart, yet we are called to be in the midst, rolling up our sleeves, getting our hands dirty, and journeying with others. We are to be united and to show in miraculous and supernatural ways the unity in the body of Christ, yet we are constantly and consistently divided. We are set apart but too often represent the status quo. Then there is this peculiarity that we are to lead as followers, direct people as servants, and point to perfection knowing that we are disastrously imperfect. We follow the One whose death gave us new life and whose life causes us to die daily. At its very core, at the heart of the matter, Christian leadership requires us to negotiate a treacherous terrain and to exhibit oxymoronic behavior.

This reality for Christian believers is coupled with the duplicitous nature of being in the world but not of the world, of becoming all things to gain one person, of pointing to perfection when we are flawed. If we are not careful, we can become like the Pharisees, Sadducees, and scribes, who resisted and opposed Jesus at every turn with their religiosity and sanctimonious attitudes. On the other end of the spectrum, we could become "practical atheists," saying that we believe in God but lacking faith, zeal, and knowledge when it comes to the church and the things of God. But, there is something between these two ends of the spectrum.

Certainly, with all of the many challenges facing the church, not the least of which is declining numbers in both membership and participation, leadership may not seem to be the most pressing issue. If there's barely anyone there, what difference does it make who is leading? Some would say that marketing is the biggest issue; others argue that it's the organizational structure and rigidity that's the problem. I've even heard that some Millennials complain that mid-morning on a Sunday is not a convenient time for church service because it conflicts with brunch and other fun activities.

In spite of the speculation about what is wrong with the church, I suggest that having a cadre of sound and dedicated leaders is at the heart of a reinvigorated and reinvented church. If the church is going to be relevant for future generations, having well-prepared and faithful followers of Christ plotting the course for local congregations is essential. There must be a core group of leaders who are committed to the work of the church and who have a keen understanding of both "from whence we came" and where we are trying to go. These Christian leaders must be able to translate current-day realities through the lens of the gospel. These Christian leaders must be willing and able to proclaim a living Savior to a dying world, even as they bear fruit that shows the transformative power of the Holy Spirit working in and through them. These Christian leaders must understand the world but not be controlled by it. They can neither be so intrigued with the world that they conform to it nor be so opposed to the world that they are unable to minister to those in it. In other words, these Christians can neither be so earthly-minded that they couldn't care less about heaven nor be so heavenly-minded that they are no earthly good.

How, then, can Christians in a modern context approach leadership in a balanced and authentic way that reinvigorates the church and moves God's people forward to advance God's kingdom on earth? I suggest that there are several foundational principles for reimagining Christian leadership in a way that goes beyond starting meetings on time and keeping them short. These principles will help us to meet the challenges of the day, develop faithful leaders, and draw others to Christ and to the church while being a welcome presence in the community and the world in which we live.

Call

Understanding the concept of "call" is one of the most important things for the church as a whole and for the individual. Many books have been written on this subject, but I believe that it is appropriate for us to think about a reinvented church by also reimagining what it means to acknowledge and accept a call from the Creator of the universe. The church has generally understood call as being something experienced only by those who consider ministry as their primary vocation even if it is not their primary source of income. However, "call" really has a much broader meaning and significance. A call is God's way of saying that there is something in us, something that God has deposited, and it is time for it to come out. There are some things that have been deposited in us that are needed for the upbuilding of God's kingdom, something that is tied to who we are created to be. This deposit was made into the depths of our souls and our being and is manifested in how we serve and minister to others. I'm reminded of Ephesians 2:10, "For we are God's handiwork, created in Christ Jesus to do good works, which God prepared in advance for us to do" (NIV). At the heart of it, a call to be a leader, whatever the title, is a call to serve God's people. It is not a call to be served by others but rather to use our gifts, talents, skills, and resources to be God's ambassadors in the world.

Knowing, understanding, and acknowledging/accepting what we have been called to do is an integral part of being a strong, faithful, and effective Christian leader. Without a sense of call, we are spinning our wheels and normally end up frustrated even as we frustrate and annoy the people around us. On the other hand, having a sense of call firmly grounds, equips, and strengthens us to do the work that God has placed in our hands. It is the foundation on which we stand and are able to build a lasting hope.

Clarity

One of the most difficult aspects of the Christian walk is that we rarely, if ever, have detailed instructions for the journey. Although there are some things that we do know, there is a lot more that we don't. In congregational life there are many competing demands that can make everything seem important. Christian leaders must discern what the most important issues are, based on having clarity about their call, purpose, and the mission of the church in the world. Having clarity means having a firm foundation on which to stand. This means that even when we do not know all the details, we do recognize where the boundaries are and the direction in which we are going. For Christians, some things are nonnegotiable—for example, the death, burial, and resurrection of Jesus Christ. If we do not have clarity about the basis of the Christian faith, about where we draw the line in the sand, then we can be "tossed to and fro and blown about by every wind of doctrine, by people's trickery, by their craftiness in deceitful scheming" (Ephesians 4:14 NRSV).

Christian leaders must be clear about what it means to be a child of the Most High God, and there must be a solid understanding of the Christian faith. This understanding comes from practicing spiritual disciplines such as prayer, fasting, and studying the Scriptures—the Old and New Testaments. It also comes from being an active part of a community of faith—yes, a member of a local congregation.

My daughter and my son are avid soccer players. They have played since they were very young and love the sport. As they have grown, not only have they learned the fundamentals of the sport, but also they have learned the language. They know the positions. They know the rules of the game. They know who is supposed to be doing what and when they are supposed to be doing it. They not only play on a team but also attend camps and skill-building clinics to improve upon the fundamental skills that they have learned. In addition, not only do they play soccer, but also they watch it on television. They watch others play the game. They watch the best of the best execute the drills that they practice with precision and excellence so that they can be better as well. In the same way, being a part of a community of faith helps us to learn the language of faith. It helps us to build upon our fundamental understanding and begin to learn from others who are practicing the faith. Leading without clarity is like trying to win a game without a game plan. Christian leaders must have clarity about those things that will not change—the fundamentals of the faith, their call and the direction, purpose, and mission of the church. Just as each soccer player knows her or his position on the field, a Christian leader's call will help to determine what her or his assignment is. In addition, knowing Scripture provides the foundation and game plan for the way forward. Practicing the faith and exercising the fundamentals will allow us to walk in purpose and fulfill the mission of the local congregation and the church in the world. Without clarity, we are more easily swayed and distracted by things that have no relevance or significance for the work that God has placed in our hands.

Character

A historic church in a large urban area was seeking a new pastor to lead their congregation. One candidate was particularly charismatic and seemed to be exactly what they were looking for in a new pastor. He showed up with his wife for one of the interviews, and by all appearances he had a model family and ministry. Some members searched the internet and found out that he was not quite who he presented himself to be. But, the church offered him the job to lead the congregation. Months after his installation as their new pastor, he had a different wife than the one who was there with him for the interview. A year or so later he was facing criminal charges for assaulting someone. Several years later, church membership had dwindled, and the church was in turmoil.

Both the church and the world are desperate for Christian leaders who have character. With so many world leaders falling because of scandal, even those outside the church long for church leaders to be different. It is not enough for someone to be gifted or to be able to express with great clarity and authenticity the mysteries of the faith. It is also not enough for someone to be dynamic or charismatic. There is absolutely nothing wrong with being gifted or dynamic or charismatic, but those qualities are not the same thing as being a person with character and integrity. Gifts are not fruit, and charisma is not character. This is not just my opinion; it is backed up in Scripture. The apostle Paul says, "The gifts and calling of God are irrevocable" (Romans 11:29 NRSV). Someone can use her or his gifts freely and be a tremendous blessing to the body of Christ, but that does not mean that the person is spiritually mature or exhibiting the fruit of the Spirit, which, according to Galatians 5:22-23, is love, joy, peace, forbearance, kindness, goodness, faithfulness, gentleness, and self-control. Being gifted does not preclude us from falling into sinful behaviors and attitudes, nor does it prohibit us from being mean and nasty individuals.

We hope that someone who is a Christian leader is also someone who has been transformed by the Holy Spirit. We hope that someone who is a Christian leader exhibits the fruit of the Spirit. Sadly, that is not always the case. What happens continually in our churches is that we mistake a person's gifts for their character. We assume that because someone can preach great sermons or pray impressive prayers, this person walks with integrity and tries to do the right thing. More often than we'd like to admit, we are wrong about this assumption. Consequently, disingenuous and duplicitous people who seek to take advantage of God's people or who have no intentions of living by God's precepts are given positions of authority in the church. These are people whom I call "jokers." One of the most critical issues for the church moving forward is to have leaders who are not jokers. Jokers are the church leaders who steal the money, not by accident of accounting but by a scheme that they devised. These are the church leaders who "run" through the church, engaging in inappropriate relationships with numerous parishioners, causing havoc and divisions in the church.

Lack of character coupled with possession of authority in the church equals a mess. This is why it is vitally important for churches to be both discerning and meticulous about those whom they ask to be in leadership; not only to be persuaded by the gifts that they see, but also to watch for evidence of the fruit of the Spirit and spiritual maturity. In addition, due diligence is more than securing permission to conduct a credit report and checking the references listed by the candidate. It means doing a criminal background check (especially for those working with children and vulnerable populations) and psychological examinations as well. But, it is even more than that. It is taking the time to look beneath the surface and to discern whether or not the person is someone who has character and integrity and is open to the transformative power of the Holy Spirit operating in her or his life. As Christians, all of us are sinners saved by grace. And, yes, we struggle sometimes to do what we know is right. However, we should be able to testify that we "used to be" this or that. There should be some evidence somewhere that our lives are changed and changing.

It should also be mentioned that there are people who are gifted and have potential but are new to the faith. I am not suggesting that people who are in this category should be excluded from serving in leadership roles. However, I am saying that being gifted is not a stand-alone criterion for Christian leadership. Gifts must be coupled with character and spiritual maturity. For developing leaders, churches must take seriously mentoring relationships and creating opportunities for growth. There must be a plan for the growth and development of all leaders—something that goes far beyond simple training in how to run meetings and greet first-time visitors. There must be a spiritual plan and intentionality about developing Christian leaders who fully operate in their gifts that God has so freely given to them while they develop new skills and grow spiritually.

Character is important for Christian leaders and is essential for a reimagined and reinvented church. While the unethical church leader who steals the money or who sexually abuses a child seems like an old story, it is one that gets replayed over and over again with different names, places, and churches attached to it but with the same impact on the individuals and congregations involved as well as the community. Churches must take seriously the "community" aspect of "faith community" and ensure, to the best of their ability, that Christian leaders build their character as they also build their knowledge of God and the congregation.

Courage

I am always struck by the number of times in the Bible that the issue of fear comes up. Repeatedly, biblical characters are encouraged not to be afraid. Abram (Abraham), Joshua, Jeremiah, and Elijah are all told to fear not. Moses encourages the people of Israel throughout the exodus story and in the wilderness not to be afraid. Deborah pushed Barak to overcome his fear and fight Sisera. The Lord tells Gideon not to be afraid, for he will not die even though God has instructed him to reduce his army of twenty-two thousand to three hundred. Esther conquers her fears and pleads with the king on behalf of the Jews whose lives were being threatened by a decree that sought to annihilate them. The angel of the Lord tells Joseph not to be afraid of Mary's pregnancy. And, Jesus lets the disciples know on more than one occasion that they need not be afraid. The point is that leadership requires courage, especially for those who are attempting to do anything on God's behalf. This is as true now as it ever has been. In spite of the fact that the challenges are different for each generation, courage is always a requirement. This is because being a Christian means being countercultural. It means speaking truth to power and going against the status quo. There will always be Pharaohs. There will always be Pharisees, Sadducees, and scribes—those who oppose God and the ways of God for their own selfish gain. Regardless of the response of others or whether or not it is convenient to do so, Christian leaders are to represent the truth about God in all situations and circumstances.

Yet, it seems as if courage is hard to come by. Whether within the walls of the church or in the public square, courageous voices and actions are atypical. While there is a difference between being courageous and being uncooperative, Christian leaders cannot just go along to get along. Our standards are higher as we attempt to represent Christ in our words and actions. I remember being on staff at the National Council of the Churches of Christ in the USA (NCC) when we were considering issuing a statement calling for the resignation of a high-ranking government official. Other Christian and faith-based organizations had already released statements, and we were being asked about our position on the issue. The late Rev. Dr. Robert W. Edgar was the general secretary at the time. On a conference call, we were weighing the pros and cons of whether or not we should denounce this official who was a member of one of the NCC's member denominations but who had taken positions that the council stood firmly against. At the time, there was a lot of pressure to come out with statements that were daring enough to get you an interview on the nightly news. I was one of the people who did not think that the NCC should call for this person's resignation, even though I did think that the person should resign. After hearing all of the comments, Bob Edgar did something that I will always remember. He said, "I need to go and pray about this." He hung up the phone, ended the call, and went into his office to pray. He called me back later that day and said something to the effect of, "I think you're right. We shouldn't issue a statement." It was a bold and courageous move that went against what others were doing and even what was expected of him, since he had been openly criticizing the actions of this official. However, instead of publicly opposing the person, we ended up issuing a statement opposing the actions and decisions that were made that we opposed—a very different thing. Bob certainly could have just done what everyone else was doing and what was expected of him. However, he took the time to try to discern the right way to move forward and then acted on what he believed was right based on his understanding of how to be God's witnesses in the world. Bob made his decision based not on his personal opinion, but rather on what he thought was the proper Christian response to the situation.

The example of Bob Edgar shows an act of courage, but there are far too many instances when cowardice has won out. Christian leaders have bowed to outside pressures to take a certain position, support a particular cause, or do something that was not quite in sync with what they espoused to believe. In one instance, the leader of a Christian organization decided to move forward with presenting a national award of recognition to someone who was found out to be physically and verbally abusive to his wife. Since the award recipients had already been announced, it was decided that it would be bad publicity to revoke it, particularly since this person had strong ties within the faith community. Although even the strongest, most grounded leader can have a moment of timidity or misjudge a situation, Christian leaders must have a courageous posture and outlook.

The other thing that is important to remember about courage is that God does not send us without help. In each instance in the Bible when someone is told not to be afraid, there is also reassurance that the person will not be alone. We go on God's behalf knowing that we are not by ourselves. We can have courage because we are representatives, not the ones in charge. It is God's work, and God is able to do exceedingly abundantly above what we can ask or think. If that's the case, our fears are miniscule in comparison to what God is able to do in order to help us complete every assignment and every task entrusted to us.

Conviction

Another key principle for Christian leaders is conviction. There are two ways conviction should be understood in terms of Christian leadership. The first is for us to have conviction about our purpose, role, and mission. Authentic leadership requires firmly held beliefs about Christ and building God's kingdom on earth. For Christians, that conviction rests on our belief that Jesus Christ died for our sins so that we could be reconciled to God. Conviction is part of having a solid foundation and prepares us to do the work that God calls us to do. Our conviction fuels us to have the drive and passion to be God's ambassadors in the world. It helps us to love God's people with an *agape* (unconditional) kind of love that makes us a light in dark places.

One misconception is that to have conviction means to be rigid and unyielding. However, conviction does not require inflexibility when working with others or when adjusting methodology to fit the circumstances or current-day realities. Inflexibility often makes it more difficult for us to act on our convictions because it makes us determined to do things only a certain way, regardless of whether or not that way makes sense or is effective. But, being dogmatic or obstinate is not synonymous with having conviction. Conviction is also not the same thing as condemning others who do not agree with us. Rather, conviction has to do with our steadfast beliefs about who we are as God's children. Having conviction means that we are fully persuaded about Jesus Christ being the Son of God and the Savior of the world. Conviction helps us to have clarity and to be unambiguous about our tasks and goals. Conviction grounds us and helps us to discern and make decisions about the way forward based on our beliefs. Consequently, those around us are better served because they can also be definitive. Conviction is not a guarantee that everything will go as planned, but it will make the plan that you do have consistent with biblical principles and mandates. In many ways, conviction serves as a kind of compass that keeps us on course and moving in the right direction.

On the other hand, lack of conviction causes disarray and sends mixed messages that diminish a leader's credibility. The leader without conviction is more easily influenced by worldly things. Without conviction, authentic Christian leadership is befuddled with equivocation and doubt. An example of this is when an international denominational body had identified another religion as being a cult. This information was on their website and in written materials. The decision was then made to remove all references to this particular religion being a cult in information that they disseminated. It is possible that one of three things happened to warrant this change: (1) the religion was never a cult but was deemed as such by this denominational body because they held a different belief system; (2) the religion is still a cult but somehow became more acceptable to the denominational body; or (3) dialogue and relationship-building created better understanding between the two groups. While it is entirely possible that another scenario or combination of scenarios account for the change, there is a major problem with the denominational body's shift in thinking. The shift happened to coincide with a national political election in which the candidate that the national denominational body supported was an adherent of the religion that was once considered a cult. This action left many to question whether or not the perspective about the religion changed for political, rather than theological, reasons. Would this denominational body change other strongly held beliefs for political gain? There was certainly some concern about what their convictions were as a result of the timing of this particular change in perspective.

The other way that conviction makes a difference in the life of Christian leaders is not only to live with conviction, but also to be convicted by the Holy Spirit when we are off course and headed in the wrong direction. To say that none of us is perfect is a profound understatement. How we deal with our imperfections is a sign of our maturity, leadership ability, and effectiveness. Yet we cannot do what we want, when we want, how we want, without boundaries or limitations. We are absolutely covered by God's grace when we make mistakes. However, the words of the apostle Paul to some misguided members of the church at Corinth echo in my ears, "'I have the right to do anything,' you say—but not everything is beneficial. 'I have the right to do anything'—but not everything is constructive" (1 Corinthians 10:23 NIV). There are parameters within which Christian leaders should operate. Unfortunately, there are far too many instances of Christian leaders who have sinned against God and God's people yet seem to be unrepentant. Consider the church leader who knows his or her proclivity for pedophilia but volunteers for vacation Bible school or to work with the children on the Easter play. Or the person who is tempted by the love of money but is always vying to count the offering or be the chair of the trustees. These are obvious examples and ones that we pray are not happening at our church. However, these kinds of violations and more severe ones do occur at churches regardless of denominational affiliation, size, racial/ethnic makeup, or location. There are also other offenses that harm the body of Christ and taint Christian leadership. Gossip, manipulation, and spiritual abuse (using Scripture and/or church tradition out of context for personal gain, to control someone, and/or to justify abusive behavior) are other ways that church leaders can lead parishioners astray. But when a church leader has embraced the transformative power of the Holy Spirit working and operating in her or his life and is convicted when in error, it is much easier to correct those mistakes before they become problems or escalate into church splits or criminal cases.

As I mentioned earlier, all of us are a former something, and we used to do this or that. Mistakes are a part of the Christian's journey. But sin is no longer our address, even though we do take a detour once in a while. For Christian leaders who have conviction and are fully persuaded by the power of God that works in and through us, feeling convicted when our words or actions are inconsistent with God's intentions for us is a part of our growth process and spiritual maturity. In this sense, the purpose and necessity of conviction for Christian leaders is that it stops us in our tracks and brings us to a place of repentance. Being convicted turns us away from sin and toward God. It keeps us humble before God and constantly seeking to do what is pleasing in God's eyes, not our own or those of others. Furthermore, being convicted elevates our behavior, actions, and attitudes to meet the standard set by Christ, not by the world.

Commitment

In a conversation with my daughter's soccer coach, Don Blanchon, we began to discuss some of the challenges facing leaders in general and church leaders in particular. Coach Don, who is also the executive director of Whitman-Walker Health, a community health center in Washington DC, made a very poignant observation. He said that in today's environment a lot of people are "commitment-phobic," making it hard to get them to volunteer for anything on a long-term basis. Churches and other nonprofits that depend on volunteers must then create ways for people to get and stay involved that only require short-term commitments. This is problematic for the church, both from a practical standpoint and from a spiritual one.

Being a Christian requires commitment. It is an individual's commitment to live by God's precepts as understood through the lens of Scripture and through Christ. It is also a collective commitment that is experienced through the community of faith. Initially, Christians make a commitment through baptism and church membership to help build God's kingdom on earth. Their commitment is a part of their confession and acknowledgment of faith in Jesus Christ. That fundamental commitment grows and dictates using one's time, talent, and treasure to benefit God's people. The work of the church is done largely by volunteers. Reluctance to volunteer or commit to serve works against the overall goal of Christian discipleship. If those who have committed to Christian discipleship are not also committed to live out that relationship by sacrificing and giving of themselves to benefit others, then we are being counterproductive and inhibiting the advancement of God's kingdom.

Similarly, Christian leaders must be willing to commit to work in ministry and serve God's people. Perhaps in some ways this is not a new problem. Jesus told his the disciples, "The harvest truly is plentiful, but the laborers are few" (Matthew 9:37 NRSV). Nevertheless, for those who are called to serve in leadership, commitment is required.

Foundational to leadership in the context of Church life is that we serve others, not expect others to serve us. The commitment, then, is to be willing to do what no one else wants to do, to be in the "underbelly" of ministry with others where things get messy. Despite the numerous Hollywood-style portrayals of ministry, the reality is that serving other people when they are most vulnerable sometimes is unpleasant. Calling on people in hospitals and nursing homes, feeding those who are hungry, visiting those who are incarcerated—these ministry activities reap their own reward but are not glamorous. When we devote ourselves to the work, deny ourselves, and pick up our cross to follow Christ, God is pleased with us and deems us faithful servants. That takes commitment.

It should be noted that being overly committed is just as bad as not committing at all. The number of the hours in the day are not going to change, nor are the number of days in the week. There is this tendency, however, to cram as many meetings and activities as possible into the course of a day and week. Many Christian leaders fall into the trap of confusing being busy with being effective. When we are overly committed, we cannot give our all to any one thing. Commitment also means discerning where our gifts are most needed and focusing our attention and resources on that.

Ultimately, commitment means showing up when we don't feel like it and when it's inconvenient. It's coming early, staying late, and filling in the gaps where needed. In a reinvented church, I imagine that it's being committed to work through uncertainty, unpopularity, and constant change when others are ready to give up. It's thinking creatively about solutions and approaches that will meet the needs of God's people. It's being present, engaged, and involved in the lives of others to make a difference. It's envisioning and working toward a brighter and more hopeful future such that it will be on earth as it is in heaven.

Compassion

Several people are credited with the saying "Be kind, for everyone you meet is fighting a hard battle." Regardless of its true source, this saying hints at the fact that we never know what someone is going through at any given moment. Church folks are masterful at covering up and disguising it when they are going through a difficult time. Spiritual clichés often mask hidden and deeply rooted problems such as financial hardships, marital problems, debilitating diseases, abusive relationships, suicidal thoughts, depression and other mental health issues, addictions, and a vast array of other troubles. Indeed, Christians have to deal with the same problems as those outside the church. There is no exemption for Christians from experiencing trials and heartache. In fact, just the opposite is true. Troubles are part of the human condition, yet sometimes it seems that Christians can be the most condemning and unsympathetic people. If we are honest, we must admit that we are sometimes more willing to give advice than to give a helping hand or even just listen to someone else's story. We make a lot of assumptions about people and their situations. Then we base our response on those assumptions, which are sometimes inaccurate. In addition, at times we are the first, rather than the last, to throw stones at the person caught doing wrong.

The essence of leading as a Christian, it seems to me, is to have compassion for God's people. How can we belittle those who face the same trials that beset us? How can we serve those whom we hold in disdain? Having compassion for others is an expression of God's love for us. Lamentations 3:22 says, "Through the LORD's mercies we are not consumed, because His compassions fail not" (NKJV). When we embrace this great love that God has for us and the ways in which God's grace and mercy have seen us through dangers seen and unseen, we are compelled, I think, to be compassionate toward others.

A good friend of mine taught herself how to crochet when her mother became sick. She would sit with her mother for hours, and crocheting was soothing for her. Robin's first project, once she got the hang of it, was to crochet a scarf for her mother. When her mother died, Robin continued to crochet and began making scarves for women at a shelter for survivors of domestic violence. She also started crocheting squares as a gift of encouragement for others. On these squares she attaches a note that simply says, "Jesus wept." She sent one of these to me after my father died. It was a reminder that Christ was with me in my mourning, and that I would get through it. It also captures the heart of Jesus, who encountered people in the midst of trials and met their most pressing needs. Jesus healed the sick, raised the dead, gave sight to the blind, delivered people plagued by demons, and saved the life of a woman caught in adultery. Jesus stilled a raging storm so that his disciples would not be afraid. Jesus wept.

Jesus had compassion for people and showed the greatest compassion when he died on a cross for our sins. Therefore, Christian leaders are charged with exhibiting compassion for others, regardless of the person's situation. Compassion doesn't mean compromising our beliefs or ignoring a situation when someone has sinned. Instead, showing compassion when someone is hurting, whether it is a self-inflicted wound or one imposed by someone else, is a reflection of Christ. Even a rebuke can be couched in love and demonstrate God's grace and mercy toward us.

Perhaps what concerns me most is that often the message from local congregations, denominational bodies, and individual Christians is one of reproach not compassion. For this, countless people have left the church and wanted nothing else to do with Christians. Rather than lifting up Christ so that people will be drawn to him, church leaders who lack compassion often end up ostracizing people from the church. A reinvented church demands Christian leaders who meet hurting people in their place of vulnerability and serve as a ministry presence for them in their situation.

Care

Christian leaders not only must take care of others, but they also must take care of themselves. Numerous studies have shown that pastoral leaders in particular are in the worst health of any of the helping professions. They are generally overweight, overworked, and suffering from exhaustion. It is also not unusual for a pastor to die before retiring from ministry, sometimes in the pulpit (both literally and figuratively). This frantic pace of constantly doing and being all things to all people leads to burnout, poor health, stress-related illnesses, and mental anguish. In addition, Christian leaders can become impatient and apathetic when they do not take the time to care for themselves.

Old Testament scholar Rev. Dr. Judy Fentress-Williams has said that rest is a part of the created order, and when we don't take time for rest, we are working in opposition to how we were created. The reality is that church life can be bad for our health, especially if we are involved in every activity, program, and project. I know Christian leaders who are at the church every day of the week and all day on Sundays. Certainly there are times when we are at church more often. The Advent and Lenten seasons come to mind. However, being at church every day and being overwhelmed with church activities is neither wise nor beneficial.

It may be pride that leads Christian leaders to neglect rest and proper self-care. It could also be a bad habit or misinterpretation of what it means to be faithful. Nevertheless, doing the work of the church should not have us in a perpetual state of mental, physical, and spiritual exhaustion. Serving others is both demanding and taxing. Finding the right balance and creating a community where rest is valued is key. There is no badge of honor or crown of glory for the overworked Christian leader.

Reimagining Christian leadership must include rest and self-care into the life of church leaders. Clearly, retreats that are jam-packed with workshops, activities, and worship services are not the answer. And, although Sunday worship services can be restorative for the individual Christian leader, they are not the same thing as resting. Taking time to regroup and replenish outside of the walls of the church on a consistent basis is necessary in order to effectively lead inside those walls and within the community. There really is no substitute. Emerging technologies may make it possible to do more in less time or provide different options for us to get rest, but nothing will ever replace it.

Christ

Finally (in the sense of the last being first and the first being last), the most important principle for Christian leaders, upon which every other principle depends, is that the individual be a follower of Christ. It may seem obvious, but anyone who would serve effectively as a *Christian* leader must believe in the birth, life, death, burial, and resurrection of Jesus Christ as the Savior of the world. This belief stands on the assurance that Jesus Christ died for our sins so that we might be reconciled to God and have eternal life. There are many leadership experts who can offer advice and a checklist of rules and guidelines about what it means to be an effective leader. Someone can even volunteer at the church and do good things. But, for the person to be a *Christian* leader and faithful servant, belief in Jesus Christ is paramount.

As Christians, we have a goal set before us that prods us to do the work that God has entrusted to us. The ability to do that work as ambassadors for Christ means that we must believe in whom and what we are representing. What ambassador doesn't believe in the one by whom they've been sent? Anyone who is to be an effective witness, faithful servant, and authentic leader in the church must be a disciple of Christ. There are many people who've been in church and participating in church activities for a long time but have never accepted Christ into their heart. Although such a person can be skilled in leading others, something will always be missing in terms of embodying Christ-like leadership if that person isn't a believer. Therefore, the reinvented church needs leaders who have Christ at the center of their lives. Christ makes the difference in who we are, how we think, how we treat others, and how we care for ourselves. Because of Christ, our minds and our attitudes are transformed so that we can serve. Because of Christ, we have strength to endure and can help others to endure. Because of Christ, we are able to tolerate fickle, erratic, and mean people. At the very heart of what it means to be a Christian leader is Christ. Christ is the chief cornerstone on which everything else is built.

The Heart of the Matter

John 7:37-52 records Jesus having an encounter with the crowds and the authorities. He found himself at odds with the religious leaders of the day . . . again. It was the last day of the Festival of Tabernacles (Booths), a seven-day pilgrimage feast in the fall that marked the end of harvest labor. It was on this day that Jesus cried out concerning what I believe is really at the heart of the matter of Christian leadership. Jesus declares, "As the scripture has said, 'Out of the believer's heart shall flow rivers of living water'" (John 7:37 NRSV). In the end, God is always concerned with our heart. We confess with our mouth but believe in our hearts. The confession is an outpouring of the belief. Leading as God would have us lead is wrapped up in what flows from our heart. Living water provides replenishment, nourishment for the soul. Living water gives nutrients and strength and fortitude, allowing us to run on to see what the end is going to be. Living water gives us joy, peace, patience, and forbearance. I love when I want to hate. I'm kind when I want to be cruel or callous. I give when I'd much rather receive.

Chemistry tells us that water is produced when hydrogen and oxygen molecules cause a transaction that results in transformation. In the same way, belief in Christ, the living water, brings about transformation in our lives. Our transformation then causes a reaction in the world that helps to transform other people's lives and the communities in which we live: there is a new creation, with the old passing away and everything becoming new (2 Corinthians 5:17). Reimagining Christian leadership is recognizing and operating with the knowledge that being transformed by Christ brings us new life, new hope, and new possibilities for doing greater things than even he did (John 14:12).

Questions for Consideration

1. How does your church support leaders and their ongoing formation, including affirming creation of space for their spiritual lives and promoting a healthy work-life balance in their service in the church?
2. How do you as a church leader cultivate courage and conviction?
3. What transformation have you experienced in church leadership that has helped transform others?

4

PREACHING what we PRACTICE
Homiletic Pedagogy for Ministerial Preparation

KYLE BROOKS

PERHAPS THE SIMPLEST, YET MOST PROFOUND LESSON I'VE LEARNED about ministry is this: always be prepared. My grandfather, Bishop Isaac King Jr., pastor of the Pentecostal Temple Church of God in Christ since well before my birth, was and is a vigorous, thorough preacher, usually equipped with a manuscript and a keen awareness of his content, the audience, and his performance. As a child, I watched him demonstrate an ongoing mastery of the principles and practices of preaching. I was aware of his introductions, his transitions, his narrative style, his closures, and his celebrations. He was every bit an example of the fervent "black preacher," whose imagery is deeply embedded in popular consciousness. In my memory, he never arrived at the preaching moment in an unprepared state. I watched him on Saturday evenings, painstakingly writing his manuscripts by hand in clear, neat print on unlined paper. I saw the stacks of sermons, hundreds of them, neatly arranged in his office. There were no illusions that preaching was a light, easy task. I knew that preparation did not start with showing up to the pulpit. Nor was it merely a matter of having a call to ministry. Rather, preparation was and is cultivated through disciplined habits born out of intentional practice. It is what results when one's purpose intersects with one's conscious growth and development.

I realized how challenging it is to reach this intersection while listening to a sermon preached at an ordination service some years ago. The preacher for this service was one of the ministers being ordained that day. This service was the final stage in a process of examinations and interviews. These ministers were deemed fit and ready for the practices and challenges of parish ministry. The preacher came forth and delivered his sermon. Unfortunately, it was memorable for all of the wrong reasons. It was clear to me that he had picked up traits and habits of preachers I had seen before. He seemed to be thoughtful of his rhetorical style and presentation. However, his ability to present stylistic elements of preaching was undercut by his lack of preparation in biblical exegesis and homiletic structure. It was a glaring problem, especially because he did not seem to be aware of it. I was concerned that he did not seem to recognize and utilize strong homiletic practices, especially in a context that highly values effective preaching. Though the ordination board acknowledged his calling, there were clear signs that his growth and development as a preacher had not been cultivated in the same way. I was saddened because what this preacher offered was a caricature, not a picture of inspired preparation. Moreover, I wondered if anyone else noticed, and whether this was just an off day or a consistent pattern.

Anyone who has preached frequently enough has had sermons that fell flat. I can think of a few that I would never want to preach again. The problem is not that we do not deliver perfect sermons every time. No one does. Highly trained musicians will miss an occasional note; professional athletes will blow an easy play. What distinguishes them, however, is not their perfection, but their consistency. They prepare themselves in such a way that excellence is their norm. It is true that the work of ministry is not merely a professional pursuit; it is a calling and a way of life. If this is so, then it makes sense that one's preparation for ministerial work (including preaching) should be thorough and disciplined. This is an ongoing project for the preacher.

Disciplined homiletic or preaching practice doesn't just happen. Quite often, it does not happen at all. If anything, a great deal of preaching has been characterized by strong attention to style and inattention to structure and content. This is not wholly unique to any one church setting or denomination. However, I do believe that this is a particular concern for settings that have alternative models for ministerial training. For the Church of God in Christ and numerous other black Protestant denominations, formal theological education (e.g., the Master of Divinity degree) is not a requirement for ordination. Instead, the structures of ministerial training and theological education are built and maintained internally, often varying by congregation. In these settings ministerial preparation often occurs through an apprenticeship model that emphasizes the personal interaction between the seasoned mentor and the developing minister. The practice of ministerial work happens in a relational context. This model has produced a number of effective and capable ministers and has been an absolute necessity in communities where formal theological education was not (and is not) readily accessible.

In my experience, there has been tension between many who see formal theological training as an unnecessary luxury and others who believe that it is extremely beneficial, if not vital, to professional ministerial preparation. What gets lost in this debate is how both formal and informal models of theological education offer respective strengths to ministerial development. To be clear, I am not implying that either formal or informal theological education should be privileged above the other. As a product of the Church of God in Christ and a recipient of formal education in theological studies, I have a vested interest in both avenues. However, I believe that much can be gained from integrating methods and strategies from both areas in order to strengthen training for preaching. No minister arrives at ordination fully formed and endowed with all the knowledge that he or she will ever need. Therefore, it is important to contemplate how *continuing ministerial education* can be implemented in order to foster disciplined habits of ministerial practice. I believe that the work of preaching is a useful starting point. By and large, the sermon is a high point of worship in the black church, and through it the preacher operates as a primary teacher and interpreter of biblical truth in the contexts of the listeners.[1] It is absolutely vital, then, that the preacher be equipped to carry out this task, and the field of homiletics offers excellent tools for this mission.

Too often, black preaching traditions have been viewed as caricatures. The style, rhythm, and rhetorical flourishes have been exaggerated in troubling ways. Many ministers have learned to emulate these characteristics without considering the careful study that supports the preaching. As I reflect on the sermon that prompted this essay, I recognize that caricature is not always intentional. In fact, quite the opposite, it sometimes is the result of not being intentional and disciplined about the work that informs the way we perform. Tradition should inform our unique, creative works instead of merely being a template that we try to reproduce. The only way to realize the full beauty and creativity of preaching is to make space for safely exploring and sharpening our habits of practice. Good preaching is not the product of one person's effort, but rather the result of collaborative insight and communal encouragement.

The Big Idea

I once heard a professor of mine talk about the idea of changing the three feet around you. If every person concentrated on affecting the environment that immediately surrounds them, we could accomplish amazing things. I keep this idea in mind when I consider ways of tackling the problem at hand. I believe that one of the strongest aspects of the apprenticeship model of ministry formation is that it happens at the local level. The immediate congregational setting is the place where vital knowledge and wisdom are gained that help make preaching effective and true to its context. I want to offer an approach to homiletic training within the local congregation that emphasizes the communal development of the sermon and the preacher.

At the heart of this approach is a cultural shift in the way black church leadership operates from the pulpit. It is clear that the black preacher has the ability to bring about individual and communal change and, understandably, plays a central role in the worship experience.[2] At the same time, this position of influence can be problematic when it elevates the preacher in an artificial way. The responsibility of teaching and leadership is very real, but the call to do this work does not make the preacher "more than human." One could say that a divine call to ministry is an "otherworldly" event that has "this-worldly" consequences, yet the preacher is very much grounded in this world as a human being who works with and serves other human beings. The difference in responsibilities should not equate to a relational distance. The role of the preacher makes sense only in conversation with the role of the congregation. This relationship cannot be grounded in a permanent sense of hierarchy.[3]

I recall a lesson that I learned from the facilitator of my summer internship group during divinity school. The facilitator, who was a rabbi at a local synagogue, talked about the ways in which people invoke the term "shepherd" when describing church leadership. The image of a preacher as a shepherd to a congregational flock is a popular one. The rabbi informed me that most people have never actually seen how a real shepherd operates with a flock. The shepherd does not lead the way while sheep follow; the shepherd guides the flock from the rear. This position enables the shepherd to see the entire flock at once. The shepherd is a powerful influence without being a constant focal point. If the minister must be front and center during the preaching moment, it is important that the community is front and center in the minister's preparation.

My idea is to guide the homiletic training of ministers in a way that grounds them in a dialogue that precedes the "call and response" of the sermon. One advantage of my formal theological education was the opportunity to take a step back from the immediate church context in order to reflect on the events that happen there. In such times of reflection I was able to enter dialogue with people whose experiences and identities were formed in ways very different from my own. I was forced to think about the things that I took for granted in my everyday practices as a minister. I was pushed to make my private habits public. This is the kind of interrogation that I hope to facilitate for developing ministers. In his book *The Roundtable Pulpit*, John McClure expresses the responsibility of preachers to "help to recreate the church as a learning community where Christians share power and permit themselves to be instructed by one another's differences."[4] I believe that this work should be embedded in the means by which ministers are trained in the local congregation. Preaching has the power to orally redefine the world and the identities of the people who hear it. What I aim to do is place that power in the context of ministerial formation. I believe that homiletic training has the power to re-create the learning community of ministers in a way that reminds them that an individual call is still to a communal work.

What does this look like? I draw inspiration from my own course of theological education. During my Master of Divinity studies I took a seminar centered on John McClure's "roundtable pulpit" method.[5] In a given class period, the students came together to discuss a predetermined Scripture passage. Alongside the Scripture, we had various readings that dealt with a number of aspects of preaching practice, such as intercultural ministry, ethical approaches to preaching, and historical studies of preaching. Each student was charged with doing her or his own research and commentary study beforehand. We brought our findings to the class discussion and shared the results of our research with one another. After this, we brainstormed the themes and ideas that emerged from our thinking about the Scripture text and our academic texts. We took notes on each other's insights, asked questions, and challenged each other's conclusions. For each sermon, we were required to employ different models of sermon preparation. From this process, each of us wrote a sermon on the given text, with each person eventually presenting a sermon and receiving critical feedback. From this process, we each offered critiques on our individual sermons. We repeated this process until each student had researched, discussed, and composed four sermons over the course of a semester.

There are three specific impacts that this method had upon my homiletic practices. First, this method impacted my habits of preparation. My responsibility was not just to myself to finish a sermon. Rather, I was firmly embedded in a communal process of preparation. I knew that the other members of the group were counting on me to bring my unique insights. To be unprepared was to rob them of a vital part of their experience. My preparation was no longer an act of individualism; it was a commitment to unified effort.

Second, this method impacted my habits of interpretation. It is natural to look at things from a perspective that reflects our own interests and biases. But we don't simply read texts as *they* are; we read texts as *we* are. I was forced to consider how my interpretive habits were grounded in things that I just assumed to be straightforward and universal. I had to consider how my readings were thoroughly shaped by factors such as gender, sexuality, class, race, ethnicity, and educational background, to name a few. The bodies and identities that we inhabit are not universal, and I learned how to embrace the fact that a difference of opinion does not negate the value of the opinion.

Third, this method impacted my habits of reflection. It is one thing to consider my sermons after the fact; it is another thing to engage in a rich dialogue about my theological concepts, my rhetorical choices, and my interpretive schemes with a group that is informed about my full process of composition. What my classmates offered was neither empty praise nor harsh criticism. Rather, it was genuine conversation on my journey from a scriptural text to a sermonic expression. This is precisely the sort of conversation that needs to be a common occurrence in the life of the minister.

What I experienced was a reorientation of ministerial training. My work as an individual was continually placed in the context of a group effort. I was formed as a preacher in ways that were not readily possible in a strict one-on-one apprenticeship. The consequence of this is that I was exposed to a different model of enacting leadership and sharing power. I learned that my power as a minister was not grounded in wielding power over others, but rather in empowering them through a faithful witness of the gospel. That faithful account has always been found in the cloud of witnesses, among the gathering of believers. I believe that many ministers have been trained, especially in their preaching, to place the great weight (and resultant glory) upon their own shoulders. While ministers should be trained to recognize their responsibilities as leaders in service of the church, it is imperative that they equally recognize the tremendous resources of the congregation. Those resources are far-reaching and sustain ecclesial life in ways that a single person's charisma or rhetorical abilities cannot.

My plan would be to implement this sort of roundtable approach to homiletic training in local churches. If there is a critical mass of ministers in training at a single church, they could form a roundtable group. For smaller churches, they could gather their ministers together to form a group. Typically, this method is employed with a pastor engaging members of her or his congregation in small groups. However, I would modify it in order to focus first on building the community among the developing ministers. The goal would be to engender trust among them so that they can safely reveal their notions of ministry (good and bad), their fears, and their vulnerabilities. If they cannot develop transparency among one another, they will never practice it with their congregations. The idea of the roundtable is popularly known from the legend of King Arthur and the Knights of the Round Table. A roundtable has no head, and thus it implies equal status of the people gathered there. The roundtable cultivates a posture of humility and reminds those present that they are invited to serve, not to rule.

I envision changes in the way church leadership is shaped and, in turn, a change in the way churches function under new leadership. I believe that transforming the approach that developing ministers take to the key liturgical task of preaching will impact other aspects of ecclesial life. A minister who is willing to empower others' contributions to the preaching moment might be just as willing to invite the congregation's investment in numerous areas. People who know that they are heard and respected by church leadership will be inclined to lead through their own service and participation. They will have a stake in the enduring life of the church. They will recognize that they too are essential ministers of the church, whether ordained or not. Perhaps the "priesthood of all believers" means the active involvement of every person in the body, each one offering unique expertise and energy. This sounds like church that has adopted a roundtable mentality in which everyone brings something to the table in the expression of gospel witness.

Continuity: Tradition and Big Idea

What I propose is not something utterly new and unheard of. At the heart of my approach to homiletic training is a hope of counteracting worrisome trends of individualistic ministerial practice. The roots of the black church are firmly embedded in a communal sensibility. In their landmark work *The Black Church in the African American Experience*, C. Eric Lincoln and Lawrence Mamiya suggest that the hostile social conditions of life in the United States reinforced a strong sense of communal freedom and linked destiny for African Americans.[6] The black church developed under conditions that required a shared responsibility for the maintenance of physical and spiritual well-being. The gifts and talents of all were vital for the sustenance of the church body. This is a model of ecclesial unity that incorporates the varied members.

However, black churches at large have been challenged in ways that disrupt communal activity. Ironically, one of those challenges arises from a traditional strength of the church: its appropriation of the experience of the Israelites in the exodus narrative. Dale Andrews writes that the application of this history to the contemporary struggle of enslaved persons fostered both a strong corporate faith identity and a Christian folk community.[7] Without a doubt, this story has been a source of tremendous inspiration and strength. Yet, the hierarchical model of leadership that functions in this narrative has had a lasting effect on black churches. Moses' role as the leader of the Israelites during the exodus has been mapped onto leaders of black churches. He was the one who ascended the mountain of God and communicated directly with God, receiving the Ten Commandments and delivering instructions to the Israelites. He was a mediator of divine instruction and guidance. Certainly, clergy take on a great responsibility in guiding congregations through worship and life in community. However, the dynamics of Moses' relationship with God do not translate directly to the role and function of the present-day black preacher. If the Christian church comprehends Jesus Christ as the Messiah and the mediator between God and humankind, then the role of the minister is not a messianic one. The minister functions as a caretaker of an ecclesial community, but not as its savior. The particular status of a church leader can and must be recognized without transforming that status into a pedestal. If anything, the minister is called to be a leader among servants and an example whose activity in the church compels all congregants to be agents of God's will in the world. Ministers should be unique and powerful visionaries, but they must also recognize that they are charged to be the first participants in the execution of that vision. Dictation from the top must be transformed into exhortation in the midst.

In broader black culture as well as in the black church, the usefulness of fixed hierarchical leadership has passed. There is still the need for those who will take on the responsibilities of teaching, facilitation, organization, and spiritual care, but they are not the singular voices speaking to these needs. The community is able to speak about and to its needs. My suggestions for homiletic training are meant to be a way of (re)connecting to the myriad voices that compose black church communities. The modern minister must be trained in a way that fosters flexibility and adaptation, not rigid conformity. The templates that worked for our predecessors are not necessarily the ones that will work for us.

This is not to say that we cannot garner tremendous wisdom and guidance from experienced leaders in ministry. However, we are charged with the task of merging tradition with imaginative construction. We must be ready for what the church is and what it will be. To be clear, formal theological education does not make an effective minister any more than a driver's license makes an excellent driver. What it *does* provide are useful tools and knowledge that, when coupled with meaningful mentorship and experience, enhance one's ability to practice ministry effectively. At its best, theological education (formal and informal alike) pushes the thinking, feeling, and doing of developing ministers so that they are ready to handle what they expect and respond to what they do not expect.

Biblical Grounding

Both the traditions of black church life and the formal setting of the theological academy inform my ideas about revamping homiletic training at the local church level. Furthermore, these ideas are supported by robust examples throughout biblical text. First, the custom of apprenticeship has several biblical precursors. The relationship of Elijah and Elisha comes to mind. In the book of 1 Kings, Elijah comes to the forefront as a prophet. Chapters 17–19 describe his exploits, highlighting his diverse ministerial experiences. He ministers to a widow and her ailing son, attending to their material need of food and the boy's physical need of healing. He confronts the royalty of Israel, Ahab and Jezebel, and speaks against their worship of Baal, the Canaanite god. He even triumphs over the prophets of Baal and justifies his faith in the God of Israel. By the time he is instructed to take on Elisha as his protégé, Elijah is already a seasoned prophet. He places his mantle on the shoulders of Elisha, who goes so far as to slay his own oxen, preventing himself from returning to his work as a farmer. We get a picture of Elisha's radical commitment to this relationship.

In 2 Kings, chapter 2, Elijah prepares to ascend into heaven, and Elisha asks for a double portion of Elijah's spirit. It is important to note that this does not mean that he was asking for twice the power of Elijah. Rather, it is a subtle nod to the fact that Mosaic law dictates that the firstborn son receives a double portion of his father's inheritance (see Deuteronomy 21:15-17). Elisha's request underscores the intimacy of his relationship and apprenticeship with Elijah; he becomes like a son to Elijah. Furthermore, the account of his prophetic career through 1 Kings spans several decades and details encounters that bear both similarity to and difference from that of Elijah. I believe that this informs us of two important aspects of apprenticeship: (1) it orients the apprentice to the mentor's work and tradition; (2) it prepares the apprentice for situations that the mentor never encountered. To be clear, the relationship that Elijah and Elisha had is not a reproducible model. However, it is a useful illustration for how apprenticeship can function well.

It is equally important to understand how apprenticeship functions in a group context. The relationship of Jesus to the disciples throughout the Gospel accounts illustrates it well. Jesus partnered with a group of people from various backgrounds and experiences, traveling with them and allowing them to absorb not only his habits of ministry, but also his habits of life. He challenged their perspectives and assumptions on a regular basis. He taught, encouraged, and corrected them. Certainly, they did not all possess the same gifts and talents or achieve the same notoriety. They did not share the same personalities or tendencies. Nevertheless, they were able to coexist in difference and in community. They were able to perform different functions in the life of the Christian church. They broke bread together, thrived together, failed together, and learned together. What this group context exemplifies to me is the power of interdependency. Ministry is not a solo endeavor wholly dependent on individual call and skill. Rather, it is a highly interpersonal work of mutuality and recognition, of laboring alongside others and translating divine inspiration into practical, substantive life informed by the gospel.

Preaching is one of the core means by which the pursuit of this life is directly communicated in congregational settings. I believe that the best practices in this aspect of worship are honed through encounters that remind ministers of the collective work of giving witness to the work of God, even through moments of individual proclamation. In order to reframe ministerial training on the local church level, it is necessary to survey your unique setting. To that end, I offer some questions at the end of the chapter that we might ask ourselves as we begin the conversation in our own congregations.

I recommend John McClure's *The Roundtable Pulpit: Where Leadership and Preaching Meet* (excellent guidance on how leadership and preaching work together) and James Harris's *The Word*

Made Plain: The Power and Promise of Preaching (an exploration of the art, history, and methods of black preaching).[8] These are two helpful and readable texts that are useful for small group ministerial training. I also recommend starting informal, exploratory conversations about how ministers are trained and how their preaching is developed. This kind of assessment will allow you to start formulating a plan that begins the transformation of a church into a learning community. When ministers are trained to make a habit of collaborative discussion and proclamation of the word, they become more faithful, truthful witnesses to the gospel. My hope is that ministers will realize that emulating the best of their preaching traditions is not a matter of mimicking style, but rather of generating the discipline, reflection, and compositional awareness that enables preaching to best serve its congregational context.

Questions for Consideration

1. How are aspiring ministers currently trained and nurtured in my church? Why (or why not)? What are the strengths/challenges of this approach?
2. How do the current and aspiring ministers in my church understand their roles/responsibilities as ministers?
3. Do the ministers in my congregation have backgrounds in formal theological education? What difference (or differences) does this seem to make?
4. How do ministers in my congregation prepare for sermons? Do they work alone, or do they seek collaboration? What sorts of resources do they use?
5. How do ministers/congregants understand the role of the sermon in the worship experience?
6. What is the makeup of my congregation (socioeconomic status, race, educational backgrounds, ethnicity, etc.)? How does this unique makeup affect how ministry happens here?
7. How does my congregation perceive the role of ministers? Do these perceptions reinforce clergy hierarchy, or do they reflect a distribution of power?
8. What strengths/challenges are present in the preaching practices of the current and aspiring ministers? Are these challenges used as teaching opportunities, and if so, how?

9. Is critical and instructive feedback communicated about preaching ministry in my congregation? If so, how? If not, why not?

Notes

1. Stacey Floyd-Thomas, et al., *Black Church Studies: An Introduction* (Nashville: Abingdon Press, 2007), 159.

2. Dale Andrews, *Practical Theology for Black Churches: Bridging Black Theology and African American Folk Religion* (Louisville: Westminster John Knox Press, 2002), 22.

3. John S. McClure, *The Roundtable Pulpit: Where Leadership and Preaching Meet* (Nashville: Abingdon Press, 1995), 38.

4. Ibid., 20.

5. Here I wish to acknowledge the capable instruction and scholarship of two of my mentors in academics and preaching, Thomas Troeger and Nora Tubbs-Tisdale, of Yale Divinity School, whose homiletics seminar "The Roundtable Pulpit" remains one of the enduring and meaningful experiences of my divinity school career. They modeled collaborative ministerial training in a way that deeply informs my writing here.

6. C. Eric Lincoln and Lawrence H. Mamiya, *The Black Church in the African American Experience* (Durham, NC: Duke University Press, 1990), 5.

7. Andrews, *Practical Theology*, 42.

8. James Henry Harris, *The Word Made Plain: The Power and Promise of Preaching* (Minneapolis: Fortress Press, 2004).

Part II

Reinventing Community

5

REINVENTING the ONE-ROOM worship HOUSE

THERESA E. CHO

My husband grew up in Brighton, Michigan, a small suburban town outside of Detroit. In the midst of strip malls and grocery outlets there are hints of the historic Brighton "way back when" sprinkled throughout the town. One of those hints is a one-room schoolhouse built in 1885, where children in kindergarten through eighth grade were taught in the same space with one teacher. The challenges of learning in this environment were that one-room schoolteachers had to be able to teach a wide range of subjects and age groups with limited resources. The benefits were that students often progressed at their own pace and had the benefit of knowing what to expect in the next grade because they observed older students learning their lessons. The older students were also expected to help the younger ones as well.

Most one-room schoolhouses existed, and some still exist, in remote and rural areas, where space is plenty and resources are few. One may assume the same for churches as well: given the area and resources, they function like a one-room schoolhouse. But this is true not only for rural churches, but also for churches in suburbia and urban settings. As more and more churches are declining in worship attendance and as small and medium-size churches are becoming the norm, churches are becoming one-room worship houses, where all generations worship together. Worshiping together provides the opportunity to embrace the generational diversity not as a challenge but as a benefit of learning from one another. Imagine people of all ages worshiping at their own pace, learning from each other the rituals, prayers, and traditions.

Why Intergenerational Worship?

While some churches may find themselves stumbling into intergenerational worship by necessity, there are many reasons to worship intergenerationally with intention and purpose. Having children in worship challenges us to examine how we engage in worship, our faith, and with each other. They remind us that there isn't a right way or one way to worship. They remind us to be open to the spontaneity of the Holy Spirit. They remind us that God is present in the messiness of our lives. They give us opportunity to reexamine the meaning of sacred and holy. They provide us lots of opportunities to exercise patience, grace, love, forgiveness, and generosity. They remind us to worship with our heart as well as our head. They give us opportunity to broaden our acceptance of those who are different from us and challenge us. Children are a gift in worship. They remind adults that God only requires us to come as we are, to ask questions, and to remain curious. Senior adults are a gift in worship. They remind us that life can be hard, but God is faithful. And all ages in between are a gift in worship. Intergenerational worship mirrors the complex, diverse, and beautiful image of God and God's creation.

Worship is a place where we as Christ's followers can practice how to live in a way that God intends for us; can experiment multiple ways of exercising grace, love, and forgiveness; and can explore the many dimensions of being in relationships of accountability. These opportunities of practice require a worship environment that is open to exploration, authentic to the needs of people, and safe for them to try something new and make mistakes. As parents, we do this with our children, or at least we should. We provide opportunities for them to learn from their mistakes and to explore the range of their personality, and we guide them in ways that may spare them from tremendous harm. Sometimes we may protect them too much and therefore deprive them of learning and discovering valuable insights on their own.

Gever Tulley, founder of the Tinkering School, asks us to imagine a world where "we have finally rounded every corner, hidden all the knives, and put safety rails around every gully and tree, where all the floors were nonskid, and pointy scissors are given only to those with driver's licenses."[1] Would we be safer? Tulley further questions whether what happens when protection becomes overprotection. How will children learn how to judge risk for themselves, learn to problem-solve, cultivate curiosity and wonderment? In his book *50 Dangerous Things You Should Let Your Children Do*, Tulley suggests experiments with space to write down field notes of observations and ways to improve. Has worship become too overprotected in the ways we engage with our faith, where tradition, rules, appropriate behavior, and structure supersede the allowance for spontaneity and freedom to explore? Much like children, worshipers should be provided opportunities to risk, discover, and tinker with their faith. If worship isn't a place where one can tinker with faith, then where does it happen?

In my church, as in many churches, I can no longer assume that those sitting in the pews are familiar with Bible stories such as Noah and the ark, Jonah and the whale, the prodigal son, or the feeding of the five thousand—stories that I heard as a child growing up. I am also keenly aware that one hour of Sunday school is not enough time for kids to build a solid foundation for their spiritual formation. Yet parents oftentimes feel ill-prepared to be the ones to teach their children the Bible, instead relying on the church to do it, and hoping that the church will.

The challenge is addressing this issue. I find it almost impossible to find a time when families can meet for a family Bible study. I am often competing with hectic schedules of school activities, games, and family events—not to mention my own. The one time I knew that people showed up was the time of our main worship service. If this is the only guaranteed time when kids, families, singles, young, old, retired, busy, college-age, cradle-age, and new-to-the-faith were going to be in one place, then I was going to take advantage of it.

More families and people are looking for churches where they feel comfortable worshiping together. Not all children feel comfortable separating from their parents to attend Sunday school, especially if they are visiting for the first time. Parents also want to feel welcomed to worship with their babe-in-arms and not feel pressured to be segregated to the nursery or a soundproof glass enclosure.

What Is Intergenerational Worship?

Is intergenerational worship merely people of all ages being able to worship together? The simple answer would be yes. But it's more than that as well. It's more than just tolerating the noises of children. It's recognizing that whether we are children or adults, we all have different needs and comforts in worship that need attending. How, then, is worship inclusive and exclusive? What in worship is meaningful and mundane? How are you breathing new life in worship?

Intergenerational does not mean kid-friendly. It means making room for those who are introverted/extroverted, cerebral/tactile, able/less-abled, and young/old to enter into worship as they feel comfortable. Whether one is an adult or a child, we all have those qualities about us. Intergenerational worship encompasses the full diversity spectrum of the congregation. Not only does it address the young, old, and everything in between, but also it addresses the young in faith as well as those who have grown up in church all their lives. It includes interfaith families who are trying to navigate both culture and faith traditions. It includes those who learn audibly versus visually or tactilely.

Worshiping as an intergenerational community pushes and challenges us to be aware of how all in worship experience God's presence. It certainly is not easy. It is challenging to plan a worship service that is intellectually stimulating for the adults and spiritually meaningful for the kids. Often the trap that churches fall into is either dumbing down the message or inserting kid-friendly moments like children's sermons. Unfortunately, this rarely satisfies anyone.

How to Worship as an Intergenerational Community

Before I went to seminary, I graduated with a Bachelor of Science degree in chemistry. I was also a teacher for children with autism. The tools and skills that I acquired in science and teaching have been helpful in moving toward an intergenerational worship. Change is an everyday occurrence in the field of science and education. The whole system is designed around observing change and its effect. As a scientist and a teacher, I know that the environment is constantly changing around us and therefore we must adapt and understand what and why the change is happening. When changes are made in worship, it can cause unsettled feelings to arise. But what if we took a more disciplined approach similar to that of a scientist or teacher?

Scientists routinely state an unknown and perform a disciplined experiment to test that unknown. Disciplined experiments are designed to be conducted in a finite amount of time in order to observe changes and effects on their identified unknown. What if we entered into a time of disciplined experiments where we would make some intentional changes to the way we worship and observe how the changes affect the people's experience? By doing so, we may get a clearer idea of what needs to actually change. If we were to conduct a disciplined experiment on ways to worship intergenerationally, what would be the unknowns? Some of the unknowns at my church were (1) the needs of families during worship; (2) what families valued as meaningful worship; and (3) how to make traditional worship accessible to all ages.

The first steps of our disciplined experiment had more to do with letting go and removing obstacles than it did with changing and adding. We started with removing some of the pews to make room for strollers, which also created space for those using walkers. We removed the sign that prohibited food and drink in the sanctuary so that kids could have immediate access to their snack crackers and juice boxes, which in turn allowed adults to have immediate access to caffeinated beverages. The next steps were relocating items in our worship experience to make them more accessible. Two big relocations that made a huge impact were moving the nursery closer to the sanctuary so that parents could be in close proximity to their children, and moving the coffee and fellowship time from the far and distant Fireside Room to the narthex so that visitors felt more comfortable to stay longer to be greeted and welcomed. Simple changes such as these created space and room for bolder changes to happen.

In order for those bolder changes to take place, I harkened back to my days as a special education teacher, where I created an

Individualized Education Program (IEP) for each of my students. An IEP assesses the current level at which a student is performing, sets measurable goals, tracks a student's progress in meeting those goals, and brings in outside support to help the student meet those goals. For my church, the IEP looked something like this:

1. *Assess the current state of worship.* The worship team at my church took some time to observe how people worshiped. We took copious notes on a Sunday's worship bulletin, observing worship through the eyes of a visitor. From the moment someone walks into the church, during worship, and after worship during fellowship time, write down how you felt. Was there someone to greet you at the door and hand you a bulletin? Were you expected to know certain rituals of worship, such as when to stand, sing, or pray, or was that explained to you? Did people greet you during fellowship time? What seemed unwelcoming? What were obstacles to people engaging in worship? What were the moments when you felt uncertain, unsure, left out, engaged, or connected? It's remarkable how much hinges on the hospitality of worship and how one is invited into worship.

2. *Try disciplined experiments and observe the results.* The aforementioned observations and assessments exposed both the simple things that we could change or let go and the bolder changes that we could live and grow into. It was time to conduct some disciplined experiments. Consider the following guidelines when implementing changes to worship:

A. *Follow the liturgical season.* The best opportunities to try something new are on special Sundays such as Pentecost, Baptism of the Lord, World Communion, or during the seasons of Advent and Lent. Parishioners are more open and accepting to try something new when there is a clear theme.

B. *Provide segregated times.* This may seem counterintuitive to having an intergenerational worship, but it is okay to have moments in worship where kids and adults are segregated for a specific amount of time. My church holds an optional Sunday school lesson during the sermon time. This allows the kids to participate in parts of worship with their family and have a time that is specifically planned for them as well.

C. *Plan baptisms, Communion, and prayers to be interactive.* Allow the kids to sit up front when there is a baptism. For Communion,

I have had the kids come up and help me bless the Lord's Supper. Community prayers can be done in ways other than verbally sharing joys and concerns. Have people come forward to light a candle, or have them write or (especially for kids) draw their prayer on a card. Plan an interactive prayer station. For example, I made an interactive prayer station for preschoolers during Pentecost focused on the Holy Spirit being like the breath of God. The kids were directed to blow on one another's arms, and consider what the breath felt like. Kids could then make a paper fan and fan themselves, while thinking about how the air moved along their bodies and faces.

D. *Make the singing of hymns or songs a teachable moment.* No matter if you have an organ or a band, most people can't read music or quickly catch on to the tune. Take this opportunity to actually teach the hymn or song. Many times, my music director will teach the chorus while the choir sings the stanzas. This is a great way to build up music appreciation for both adults and kids.

E. *Evaluate and adjust your sermon and preaching style.* If your style of preaching gravitates more toward dissecting the Greek or Hebrew roots of a particular word in the Bible, consider balancing that with telling a story. Storytelling is a great way to engage people and connect your point to how they can apply it to their lives. Storytelling can come in different forms: written, verbal, or visual.

F. *Use different resources.* Because we are a small church with limited resources, we had to be creative and frugal in discovering ideas and acquiring materials. Social media such as Facebook and Twitter are very useful ways to share ideas and to network with other congregations and pastors. Often you will discover blogs and websites that are full of free resources. Pinterest can spark ideas for interactive prayer stations, crafts, and worship ideas. I often visit my local reusable art thrift store for materials. They usually have in bulk items such as candles, Christmas ornaments, paper, fabric, and buttons that are extremely affordable. I also borrow as much as I can from other churches in the area. Sharing resources lowers the cost tremendously and at the same time increases what is available to you.

The important thing to remember when doing a disciplined experiment is to try, edit, change, keep, and modify. It doesn't have to be grand. Start with figuring out what to let go of before adding anything new. And remember: change can open up possibilities that you didn't even realize were possible.

The changes that we made didn't happen all at once or even overnight. We grew into it as the needs changed. We grew into it as we adjusted to the different ways of being community. In some ways, the pastors and staff needed time and still need time to grow into it as we learn new ways of pastoring, teaching, and serving this particular church community. We are also continuously evaluating, adjusting, and observing—always measuring the pulse of the worshiping community's needs.

There is not just one model of intergenerational worship, since so much depends on your context of location, church culture, and faith tradition. No matter if your worship style is traditional or unconventional, remember the following:

1. *Provide different entry points into worship for all ages.* Whether an adult or a child, everyone has a different comfort level in worship. So people should be able to enter into prayer, listen to a sermon, sing a song, and engage in worship right where they are—spiritually, physically, and mentally.

2. *Plan worship that is interactive and sensory.* Consider how worship involves people being participants, not just observers, and also how it involves all five senses—touch, sight, smell, taste, and hearing. Theological concepts and biblical stories can, unfortunately, be relegated to the abstract. By allowing people to engage in biblical stories interactively, we help connect their lives to God's word.

3. *Involve everyone and give them an out.* While everyone should feel invited to participate, everyone should feel just as invited to not participate, yet still feel included in worship. For example, when my church sets up interactive prayer stations, we also allow people to stay seated in the pews to sing along or meditate to Taizé songs, simple songs composed by the Taizé ecumenical community in France.

4. *Improvise.* Children in worship provide lots of unexpected moments. Sometimes these moments will come in the pitter-patter of a toddler approaching the pastor in the middle of driving home the final point of the sermon, and sometimes they will come in the loud squeal of a hungry infant during the silence of prayers. Children in worship are a guarantee that worship as planned is not going to go as smoothly as expected. These are great opportunities to hone one's skill in improvisation. The best concise rules of improvisation come from Tina Fey's book *Bossypants*.[2]

The first rule is "Say Yes." This rule is intended for when things you have planned haven't quite gone the way expected. Instead of conducting damage control, tweak the original plan. One Sunday when Communion was planned in my church, no one remembered to buy Communion bread. Fortunately, there was a minimart not far away. Unfortunately, all they had left were hotdog buns.

An add-on to the previous rule is "Say Yes, And," which means improvising is more than just being open to the unexpected. We are required to contribute, even if it is a crazy idea. Hotdog buns were certainly not the ideal Communion bread, but they did provide a great opportunity to incorporate into the Communion liturgy the everyday ways God is present in our lives and how we are to remember God in the everyday rituals.

The second rule is "Make Statements." This is Tina Fey's positive spin on the original rule of "Don't Ask Questions." In an improvisation scene with two persons, if one person is constantly asking, "Who are you? Where are we? What are we doing here?" the pressure to come up with the answers is all on the other person. Partnership and working together are essential in leading and participating in intergenerational worship so that the other person is not left to shoulder all the responsibility. Improvising the unexpected moments in worship is much easier when you know that it isn't all up to you. Creating a culture where those in worship and leading worship are able and willing to pick up the pieces when things go unexpectedly is a great example of practicing community.

The last rule is "There Are No Mistakes, Only Opportunities." This is a great mantra for anyone leading and planning worship. Many times the unexpected moments are the most Spirit-filled moments, reminding us that God is truly present in the midst of the orderliness and the messiness of our lives. These opportunities allow us to practice grace with one another and not take ourselves too seriously.

5. *Make a covenant.* As we noted before, it's not easy worshiping as an intergenerational community. Noises from kids can be loud and distracting. There may be parts of worship that you just don't care for. These things can distract our attention from the wonderful benefits that an intergenerational community brings. Making a covenant whereby the church acknowledges the challenges and yet embraces the benefits can be a wonderful resource to all.

Unfortunately, it takes only one bad experience or dirty look to ensure that the parent holding a crying baby never comes back. A worship covenant can keep that from happening.

Beyond Worship

Intergenerational worship is more than the one hour on Sunday. Intergenerational worship is about becoming an intergenerational church. The trickle-down effect of changing worship is that eventually the structure and system of the church will change as well. To accommodate adults with children to participate in leadership of the church, my church had to consider the time, days, and length of meetings. It was not uncommon to see kids coloring in the corner at the finance committee meeting. The staff moved from a hierarchical system to a more collaborative system of decision-making. Just as we explored our faith in different ways, we explored different ways of being church. All planning was done through the lens of creating an intergenerational community.

My church's presence in the community became more intergenerational as well. Often, passersby would be invited to chalk prayers and blessings on the sidewalk. Colorful chalked drawings and sacred words from all ages would litter the sidewalk, only to be blanketed with new ones as the old ones faded away. On Saturdays we opened a food pantry to provide fresh groceries to families in our neighborhood. Many in my church were able to participate as a family on Saturday mornings together before they headed off to soccer games, birthday parties, and other family activities. During the week, we started a music after-school program with the public school across the street, inviting families who wouldn't otherwise step inside a church to come and learn music.

Intergenerational worship has its challenges, but it opens up many possibilities as well. The foundation of intergenerational worship is a willingness to risk, explore, and engage in our faith that stretches and comforts us at the same time.

Questions for Consideration

1. What are the assumptions about how children and adults worship that shape your church's worship space and format?

2. How might worship in your church free people to "tinker with their faith"?

3. What simple steps can you and your church take to transform worship into an intergenerational experience?

Notes

1. Gever Tulley, with Julie Spiegler, *50 Dangerous Things You Should Let Your Children Do* (New York: New American Library, 2011), xiv.

2. Tina Fey, *Bossypants* (New York: Little, Brown, 2011).

6

BEHOLD!
I am DOING a new THING
Rivers in the Wasteland

JAMIE P. WASHAM

I am doing something new; it's springing up—can't you see it? I am making a road in the desert, rivers in the wasteland.

—Isaiah 43:19 CJB

Prelude

YOU WALK IN THE FRONT DOORS, AND THE FIRST THING THAT HITS you is the smell. It is not the usual trappings of First Baptist Fill-in-the-Blank.[1] Instead, you smell curry, mingled with the faint funk of humanity. You pop into the kitchen. Tamara pauses and smiles, offering you a sample of her curry and roti. Although it is only 9:00 a.m., and you recently had breakfast, the cardamom-chili-cumin-cinnamon-coriander combination makes your mouth water, and you indulge—for a moment. Heart and belly warmed, you continue on, and run into Carl, one of the houseless people who receives mail and takes showers in the building's drop-in center. He brings you up to speed on his job search. The ability to have a legitimate address for applications has been helpful in the process. He brings up the storm from the night before. He mentions seeing a branch lying on a solar panel on the roof. You know that it must be cleared for the panel to function properly. Moving on toward the fellowship hall, you catch the tail end of a parent-toddler gym class. Little bodies in small clusters wind down the last of their dance moves. You hear the hoop group starting to make their way into the hall.

Upstairs, you settle in for your meeting with the pastors of the other three congregations—delivered in Karen, Haitian Creole, and Spanish. The pan-church service and potluck last Sunday went off without a hitch, but some of the children have been leaving too permanent a mark on the pews. Church elders are not amused, and you need to get together to address the behavior and a response. The collective Sunday school, shared by the four congregations, is bursting at the seams; more classroom space will be needed soon.

Afterward, heading toward your study, you encounter Jeri, who runs the free store in the basement. They need help packing and moving a house-load of donated furniture. We can have it to give away, but we will need bodies and trucks to move it ourselves. Maybe some of the teens could help.

You make it to your office and begin to settle in to work on your sermon and answer messages. You hear the strains—and sometimes it is a strain[2]—of the youth orchestra practicing in the other part of the building.

Later on, after La Leche League leaves and the senior lunch bunch migrate back home, movement takes on another pace, the space quiets. Tai chi practitioners begin to slowly and deliberately stir the air. Members of NAMI[3] begin to arrive.

Each month, and as constant as the moon, many of the urban homesteading crew, Stitchin' Klatch, take over the kitchen. With their sewing, knitting, cooking, canning, and preserving, they often spill into the fellowship hall. Many of them, and others, tend plots in the community gardens around the church building, cultivating keyhole plots, growing food and flora. Sunflowers support sugar snap peas and stand behind rainbow chard. Marigolds mingle with tomatoes, cilantro, sage, and chives.

Like symbiotic plants, people support one another as well. And so it was that several years earlier, four small churches scrambled to fit into and pay for the spaces that they had. One was an older, mostly white and shrinking congregation, with a fine facility that it no longer completely filled. Another, a Spanish-speaking church, generations strong, outgrew its existing facility and needed a bigger place, closer to where the members lived. A third church worshiped in French Creole; its members came from Haiti, the Democratic Republic of Congo, and Côte D'Ivoire. Then there were the waves of Chin and Karen families who relocated from Myanmar into town. Because everyone loves Jesus, they maintain the belief that it will work. Together, under one roof, they collectively and individually make church happen.

Since the churches came together, things were different—and not always easier. There is no shared idea of mine and yours and ours; we all changed—inside and out. The building changed—inside and out. Some will always recall when we did things a certain way, in bygone days. However, more come to serve and teach and learn, because of the way they are now.

Since members of the Karen church remove their shoes before entering the sanctuary, space shifted to accommodate shoes outside the doors. All congregations are considering removing shoes, as well as what that implies for floor surface remodeling. This is indicative of the cooperative planning underway to make the space better fit new collective and eclectic needs. We were committed to shrinking our energy use in the process. We blew insulation into the gap between the walls and exterior stone, uprooted the pews, put down zoned radiant flooring so that the heat passes through bodies before floating up to the rafters. This way, the organist could heat the zone under the organ during the week for rehearsing without heating the entire sanctuary. This is stewardship too.

Existing pews were rearranged in concentric semicircles, with more spaces for people in wheelchairs and walkers to choose to sit. There still is a version of a center aisle, for wedding ceremonies and funerals. Edges of the sanctuary make it easier to welcome children and families during services. Room was made for more instruments and musicians. Although we often did not understand one another, the confusion was not purely linguistic. However, the silver lining was that meetings ran at a different pace. We really got to know each other.

We believed that this egalitarian, common, yet distinct, church was what we were being called to become. One of our recurring questions became "What am I willing to give up in order to make this happen?"[4] Another was "What am I willing to do or what am I willing to release in order for church to be here?" We trusted that beyond our profoundest doubts God is able make a way and able to transform challenges into blessings.

In Real Life

So this sounds lovely, and almost too good to be true, because it is. The above is a fiction, but bits of it are already happening in real churches now. Individual churches are choosing to do the work of reimagining what church can be. The particular calling and implementation will differ for each church. The priorities and possibilities will be specific to each church. However, there are universal questions to consider: How can a church really make change manifest—seriously, in a real church, with real personalities, gifts, and limitations? How do you build the dream with not-so-dreamy conditions? Donald Rumsfeld, American poet laureate of war, opined, "As you know, you go to war with the army you have, not the army you might want or wish to have at a later time."[5] Likewise, you build the church with the resources and members you have, not the ones you wish you had. The challenge is how to get there from here (wherever here and there are for your community), with real people, budgets, and the rest. How do you create the kind of place where people are drawn to be and to participate? How can a church and its people move closer to God rather than limitations, fear, or self? Specifically, how does this manifest in physical church buildings?

Do most churches privilege place or people? Is it preferable to have a church building that is pristine and empty all but a few hours a week or one that is being used, and maybe abused, by many people? Which is better use of space, preserving what you have or using what you have? Is it possible to do both, to take care of people and place together?

If church is supposed to be a foretaste of heaven, then there is much to be done. Granted, it is hard to build heaven with the earthly materials at hand. Transformation is ongoing work. It means admitting where you are poor or greedy, where you grasp, and what you are willing to share, and what you hold open or firmly shut. Sometimes it requires hanging drywall or keeping weeds in check. The work of God is rarely dull or what you expect.

Proverbs 29:18 warns, "Where there is no vision, the people perish" (KJV), or "Without a prophetic vision, the people throw off all restraint" (CJB). A community must do the work of asking and listening to where it is being directed to go, before it can ever get there. There are many ways to do this, but it helps to have a plan. In an attempt to live into this idea (calling?), Underwood Memorial Baptist Church embarked on a visioning process in June 2012. Guided by the Spirit and using the model based on Jill Morin's leadership and work, *Better Make It Real*,[6] church members sought to understand what needed to be created or let go. Members of the church met together for an intense day of looking honestly at where we had come from and where we wanted to go as a church. We thought and prayed, remembered and dreamt, sifted, sorted, and arrived at six principle directions.[7]

Over the summer, groups met to imagine and discern what it would be like if these ideals were already realized. The groups named and identified specific things that could help bring the church's reality closer to the vision. We met back together at the end of the summer and collected all the ideas, arranged them—long-term, short-term, low-hanging fruit—and put them out for people to sign up to work on each one. Everyone understood, going in, that not everything would get done. An idea might be remarkable, but if no one volunteers or steps up to make it happen, then it won't happen.

Core Baptist values are autonomy of community and individual. Churches determine their own direction. Given our self-understanding and organization, this voluntary and democratic model, whereby people select themselves rather than waiting to be tapped for service, worked well for us. This process depends on each of person stepping up or opting out. That can get messy, but as Baptists, who take seriously the priesthood of all believers, where all are free to choose and are responsible for their choices, it made sense.

It took only a month for several to-do signs to come down. The work was done. The seeds that we planted are beginning to bear fruit. Slowly, things are beginning to develop. People, both the usual and unusual suspects, are showing ownership and agency.

One of the first things to happen at Underwood was the removal of one of the penultimate pews in order to make an obvious and welcoming space for children. One morning, two women, armed with drills, a headlamp, and gumption, removed the second-to-last pew on one side of the sanctuary. In its place went a rug and a rack with books and coloring pages. In the past, people with children would leave the service when their children acted like children. But the church wanted parents and children to feel welcome to stay during services, and so we created a place that made that more obvious. This is one small way that mission and belief can manifest in a physical space.[8]

Beyond the particular context of Underwood Church, churches need to begin to ask what their physical places of worship say about what they believe, and how those places shape the lived practice of those beliefs.

Church property is rife with significant challenges and opportunities. Physical space can be a drain on limited resources, or it can be used in ways that reflect a church's history and mission while maintaining sustainable, creative, and forward-thinking practices.

Place as Practice

A well-known worship song, alluding to 1 Corinthians 3:16-17, asks God to prepare the believer to be a sanctuary, a temple. The places of worship and the places where we practice our faith have always been given serious consideration and contemplation. And while the actual houses of worship are not the only such places, they are a major one for most people. Hence, it becomes very important to consider how you live your call and ministry as church, including how this is expressed through buildings and property. This raises the question of whether your attitude about structures and land supports or undermines your professed beliefs—whether place matters. Does the place that you occupy move you closer to or further away from the Spirit?

Another way to pose this question is to ask where you have had your most profound encounter with the divine. Has it been in a church, in nature, in Times Square, or Angkor Wat? Has it been in the mountains, or in an intimate moment with a loved one? Has it been in the desert, at sea, or does it occur when you inhale the scent of your child? Again, the question is, does place matter?

Church buildings and grounds may not seem particularly theological or Spirit-filled, yet consider the extensive chunk of text dedicated to building plans and maintenance provisions in the

Old Testament. 1 Kings 5–8 records and then 1 Chronicles 22–29 repeats and expands extensive, and some might say exhaustive, descriptions of temple building specifications, replete with furnishings, décor, flooring, surfacing, utensils, the rota of who would be in charge of services and upkeep, the duties of the musicians, gatekeepers, treasurers, and other officials, and their names.

Why is so much of our Scripture given over to building specifications? In part, it demonstrates that buildings have always required a lot to maintain them well. More to the point, these passages remind us that place affects us, and we affect it. All families in these chapters, and their constituent parts, however they are configured, are essential, in however they serve.

Humans did not and do not always worship and encounter God in a building. Throughout time, people have recognized and honored God in groves of sacred trees and in tents and tabernacles and formal, formidable structures. It can be easy to forget that church is not a building, but rather a people and a way. Buildings serve as expressions of and influences upon a church. They can be creative and life-giving or demanding and draining.

However, they often embody what is important for the community that worships there. Furthermore, the construction of houses of worship often requires several generations to accomplish. Perhaps this indicates an understanding that no church belongs to only one generation, a given mosque does not belong only to one age, and no temple is for all time. In many buildings the culture and beliefs of those who built it are etched, carved, and expressed in every way. And as the users of those buildings change over the years, those expressions change. The Hagia Sophia in Istanbul, for instance, maintains elements of the cathedral and mosque that it once was.

Buildings are not church, but they do affect the worship and work of the church. What do church buildings broadcast about what happens there, what the people within its walls believe, and how they live it out? How does place affect belief? Does it influence choices and priorities, or how you pray or sing or know and hear God?

Much research has been done linking physical place and healing.[9] Views of nature, actual or reproduced, have been shown to help people recover from illness.[10] Smells can similarly affect healing. Florence Nightingale famously used lavender to soothe her patients, while advocating for airy, well-lit rooms, as agents of healing. Esther Sternberg, a physician who considers the effect of place on patients' healing, contends that we can create places that contribute to healing or sickness.

Physicians and nurses know that a patient's interest in external things is the first sign that healing has begun. Our surroundings in turn have an effect on us in positive or negative ways. You help create or destroy, aid or neglect, the world immediately around you. What you do or don't do affects both the world and yourself.[11] You can create places that degrade and drain away joy, or you can create places that foster healing, sustaining the health of earth, people, and buildings.

Churches can put this knowledge to work. Churches ought to intentionally create places, within and outside their walls, that make people and communities more integrated, well, and whole. Churches can use property as massive signboards for what they are about. If the highest ideal is maintaining both the status quo and a beautiful façade, that will manifest itself. If a church is willing to take risks and try new things that will also show. What percentage of a church's resources goes to maintaining its facility? Is that the best use of resources? Investments in maintaining and improving infrastructure are important and must be weighed in the light of what they will enable the church to accomplish. An inefficient boiler adds up to bad stewardship. Ideally, a church building would generate energy and resources for a community rather than draining them away. What if churches were the places people thought to turn first to try new things and where they knew it would be safe to risk and fail and try again anew?

Thinking of place as theology and ministry means shifting your aesthetic and values. A lawn may not be the highest or most beautiful ideal. The cathedral in Cuernavaca, Mexico, is magnificent. Not only can you hear a mariachi Mass, but also you can read the gospel on its walls. In the late 1950s the church stripped away, and gave to aid the poor, the gold veneer gilding its interior. When they did, they revealed a neglected seventeenth-century mural illustrating the mission and martyrdom of Philip of Jesus (1572–1597) and twenty-three others in Japan. Threads of gold remnants still trace through the stucco mural, illuminating the story. It is more beautiful because the gold was peeled away.

The building is not the church; the church is the people. The people serve God, not a place; place acts as an extension of ministry and mission. What might you do to leave your buildings more fit for your children and future members? The persistent and urgent questions are these: What are you doing for others? What is this church doing with, within, and beyond your walls?

If you see the building territorially, as a gift that is exclusively yours and yours alone to keep or to give, then you might give hesitantly, even grudgingly, considering your options, hedging your bets, or giving from a sense of smug obligation and duty. If, instead, you see all of this as something lent to you by God and by your children, who allow use for a time, then you learn to hold with open hands and hearts, and the Spirit can flow more freely.[12]

Many communities use place in thoughtful and generous ways. Upstairs and down, from the basement to the sanctuary, Old Cambridge Baptist Church in Cambridge, Massachusetts, is filled every day of the week. It is filled with dancers from the ballet company housed there, editors and contributors for the Homeless Empowerment Project newspaper *Spare Change News*, staffers of the Ethiopian women's empowerment organization, church members, and many, many more service agencies and missions.[13] At Tippecanoe Church, in Bay View, Wisconsin, the "unchurched and dischurched" are welcomed to their contemplative life center, healing community gardens, or all-night prayer vigils that also serve as cold-weather intervention for the houseless.[14] Tikkun Ha-Ir (Hebrew for "repair of the city") is a pan-congregational, interdenominational volunteer Jewish organization in Milwaukee.[15] They expanded their sense of place beyond their own property lines. Tikkun Ha-Ir links farmers-market vendors and hungry people. Rather than throwing away produce that would not last until the next market day, vendors/farmers can be satisfied that their labors did not go to waste, while at the same time claiming a charitable tax deduction. Everybody wins. Other churches house multiple, distinct, and merged congregations, youth centers, food pantries, or meal programs. These communities, and others like them, are doing vital work through the ministry of their buildings.

Bringing the Inside Out, Carrying the Outside Within

Church structures are built to house and inspire encounters with God; make them reflect the God whom you seek! Create safe, gracious, and peaceful places of healing and life. Think of your church property as a semipermeable membrane, where theology is lived on the outside, in the building and grounds. Just as a church message board reaches each passerby, so too can property testify for (or against) the work being done inside and beyond. How might you create a semipermeable membrane between the church and the rest of the world? What are the challenges and opportunities? There may be dissenters, but proposing the conversation is worthwhile. Furthermore, having the conversation can be a way to invigorate the church.

Imagine if churches, both people and their places, were at the forefront of social change. Why do churches maintain lawns? Endless stretches of nonproductive land, fertilized to grow so that it can be cut down in its prime by a noisy lawnmower spewing fumes, seems an ill-fitting metaphor for what church is about. Why not gardens that feed the hungry and nourish the gardener? What if the lawn were productive? Abundance in this sense might look different from what the prevailing aesthetic allows. Instead of perfectly manicured hedges and lawns that no one uses, interpret beauty and prosperity to mean a landscape that is fecund with nourishing food and flora rather than chemically fertilized and crew-cut lawns. As the rallying cry of the Victory Garden Initiative, advocates of urban agriculture, puts it, "This is a grassroots movement. Move grass. Grow food."[16]

Make church a place of collaboration, vision, and possibility. Risk having a building that is more inhabited than pristine. Be the first building in the area to generate more positive than negative effluvia. Instead of sending out waste from the facility, generate energy. Install composting toilets. Collect rainwater from the roof for the gardens. Instead of sending water from the washing of dishes and hands into the city sewer system, redirect it toward the garden plots. Commit to recycle and compost instead of tossing more into the garbage bins. Harvest energy from the sun and the wind on your roof, tower, and steeple. Invest in solar panels and raise wind generators in towers and steeples. Let the Spirit move. Make the building more efficient, allowing you to better steward your resources, freeing you up to allocate more for missions and caring for the poor and the hungry and the naked. Instead of consuming resources and generating waste, create resources and generate energy.

Imagine the possibilities inherent in the surplus food and energy. What might you do with the abundance? What might you do to leave this place more fit for your children and future members? The money saved from this kind of stewardship could be transformed into God only knows what. The church becomes the place where you seek out to try new things, to get help, to offer what you have.

You can control some choices but few outcomes. Choose to open widely, to cast your bread on many waters; allow God and the world into your heart, your building, and your bank accounts. Put Spirit and people above property; risk getting worn out rather than petrifying. Open the church building as a sanctuary and mission in every sense. Move the pews around, put in radiant flooring so that the heat goes up from the floor and through your bodies, making more seats accessible for wheelchairs, allowing you to hear and see one another while you pray and speak and seek and sing. Get rid of your lawn and make way for garden plots, planned and freewill. Create lovely, labyrinthine places that are welcoming to be within. If you are hungry, come and eat. If you are passing by and have need, take or tend. This church hosts a free store; we become the place when you have something to give or when you have need. It is a space of movement, dance, meditation, stretching, rest, music, silence, filling and feeling the void. It is the place to go to give and to receive. Make the place a witness.

Make choices rooted in abundance, not scarcity, privileging people over property. Have the courage to risk following the Spirit past where you are and into where you could be. You will make mistakes. Not everything will work. But that would happen even if you did nothing new at all. If the local and broader church is willing to risk being more actively visionary, it must be willing to risk it all for the work of Christ: prestige, building, identity, and calling in its current form. You must risk being uncomfortable, stretched, and changed. You must accept that the institution, and you yourselves, will not be the same on the other side of this work. How might you actively and consciously meld practice and physical space (body and church) as deep manifestations of your core theology?

God gives remarkably specific commands to Noah about how to build the ark and what to bring on it (Genesis 6:14-16). Of all the things I would want God to provide exquisite detail about, boat-building plans would not be the first choice. Now I know why people are always building replicas of Noah's ark: it's clear what it looked like. What if we harnessed that energy and built what was needed to save us in this time and place? What is God calling us to build? It might seem simple or irrational or far-fetched, but I'm sure that Noah looked crazy—until it started to rain.

You are called to build community, with God and with one another, in specific places. Your specific place is where you are right now. How do you do that? Who is included? What is involved? What do you need to know in order to begin? Noah and his people follow God's call onto a rudderless boat; they crowd into this little floating box and trust that they will have what they need. Surrender into the truth that you never were in control to begin with. Noah had no idea where or when or if that boat would make land when he built it and set sail. Car headlights at night show only enough to get you through the darkness to your destination. Unlike Noah, you aren't building a boat to get away and save yourselves while others drown. Build a place of shelter and provision where are all welcome. How do you create community? To borrow a well-known line from the movie *Field of Dreams*, "If you build it, they will come."

Build it where you are, with what you have now. You don't need to have it all figured out in order to begin. You do need open hearts, the courage to be imperfect, and love for God, one another, and yourselves. You don't need all of the "Why?" questions answered, as satisfying as that might be. Do take inventory of who you are, where you've been, and where you hope to go. Love wastefully.[17] Continue to remind yourself and each other what you've done together, and how, and for what and for whom.

I am the LORD, who opened a way through the waters,
  making a dry path through the sea.
I called forth the mighty army of Egypt
  with all its chariots and horses.

I drew them beneath the waves, and they drowned,
  their lives snuffed out like a smoldering candlewick.
But forget all that—
  it is nothing compared to what I am going to do.
For I am about to do something new.
  See, I have already begun! Do you not see it?
I will make a pathway through the wilderness.
  I will create rivers in the dry wasteland.
The wild animals in the fields will thank me,
  the jackals and owls, too,
  for giving them water in the desert.
Yes, I will make rivers in the dry wasteland
  so my chosen people can be refreshed.
I have made Israel for myself,
  and they will someday honor me before the whole world.

—Isaiah 43:16-21 NLT

Postlude

On your way out of the building, you pass the wooden doorframe where a young person recently carved her initials. When it first happened, cooler heads did not prevail, yet now, each time you see it, you lift her in prayer. Perhaps it is the imperfections that make us all more precious. You walk out of the building. Dusk is falling. People are beginning to arrive for the overnight vigil, where houseless persons are known to linger and often sleep. (Who among us hasn't nodded off in prayer?) Coffee is brewing for the Alcoholics Anonymous meeting. You hear laughter and last notes as the hand bell choir packs up after rehearsing.

Passing the garden, you pinch off some basil and harvest a few tomatoes for supper, and you take a few sprigs of lavender for your bedside. You step onto the sidewalk, taking the church with you.

Questions for Consideration

1. Does physical space drain your church's resources, or is it used in creative ways on behalf of the church's mission? Or a little bit of both? How so?

2. What stories of abundance shape the work and mission of your church? What stories of scarcity shape your church?

3. What risks would your church like to take? What risks would you like your church to take?

Notes

1. This is a composite of many churches, past and present, extant and imagined, doing amazing things. The following list could not be exhaustive, but these are a few of the communities that have inspired, directly or subtly, this vision: Old Cambridge Baptist, Hyde Park Union, Underwood Memorial Baptist, La Iglesia de la Puente de Cuzcatlan, First Baptist Waukesha, North Shore Baptist, First Baptist Lynn, First Baptist West Allis, Catedral de Cuernavaca, Tikkun Ha-Ir, Crestview Baptist, Thyatira, Sardis, Laodicea. . . .

2. If you've ever listened to someone learn to play an instrument, you know that for every awkward trumpet, oboe, and viola in progress, there come utterly unexpected and brilliant moments of transcendence and grace.

3. The National Alliance on Mental Illness (website: http://www.nami.org/).

4. Rev. Deborah Davis-Johnson, pastor of Williston-Immanuel United Church in Portland, Maine, and her church repeatedly asked this question during their merger with a sibling congregation.

5. "Troops Question Secretary of Defense Donald Rumsfeld about Armor," *PBS Newshour*, December 8, 2004 (http://www.pbs.org/newshour/bb/military/july-dec04/armor_12-9.html).

6. Jill J. Morin, *Better Make It Real: Creating Authenticity in an Increasingly Fake World* (Santa Barbara, CA: Praeger Publishing, 2010). Here I wish to express my deepest gratitude to the members of the Underwood Church, who are doing this work so imperturbably, cheerfully, and well, and to Jill Morin for her skillful Sherpaing of the community through this process.

7. At Underwood Memorial Baptist Church, we determined together to set our aim as follows:

    a. Foster a spirit of ongoing and consistent service for all and from all in our church, city, and world.

    b. Grow and maintain our social, learning, and musical opportunities for all ages.

    c. Be a financially secure church that lives/acts with a spirit of abundance.

    d. Update/improve our physical environment to enhance experience of church and reduce costs.

    e. Increase awareness of our history/legacy among our members; bring what's inside the walls outside.

    f. Have a plan for attracting and retaining a diverse membership.

8. Two, now middle-aged, former youth of the congregation walked in during funerals in the past year, and each said, "Wow! It looks just the same!" and I thought, "Really?" Each commented that on later reflection, something less tangible had shifted, but the fact remains that the physical space has long remained static. I'm not advocating change for its own sake, but neither am I a proponent of maintaining the status quo because that's the way things have always been. Essentially, be mindful of how a place is or is not serving the mission of the church.

9. See Esther M. Sternberg, *Healing Spaces: The Science of Place and Well Being* (Cambridge, MA: Belknap Press of Harvard University Press), 24.

10. For more on this, see Roger Ulrich's work on evidence-based design, and also Ann Devlin and Allison Arneill, "Health Care Environments and Patient Outcomes: A Review of the Literature," *Environment and Behavior* 35, no. 5 (2003): 665–94.

11. Sternberg, *Healing Spaces*, 290–91.

12. Inspirited by Roberta Porter from her poem "Grace in Giving."

13. Website: http://www.oldcambridgebaptist.org/.

14. Website: http://www.tippechurch.org/.

15. Website: http://www.thi-milwaukee.org/.

16. Website: http://victorygardeninitiative.org/.

17. John Shelby Spong is the first person I heard issue the invitation to "love wastefully."

7

NOT your GRANDMOTHER'S holiday BAZAAR

Ecumenism for the Twenty-first Century

LAURA MARIKO CHEIFETZ

I USED TO HATE THE KIDS PRAYING IN A CIRCLE AROUND THE FLAG-pole—me, the Christian. I was a double pastor's kid by the time my best friend and I walked past a large cluster of our high school classmates holding hands, heads bowed. My dad was serving a Presbyterian church. My mom was serving a Congregationalist church. I counted my year by liturgical seasons. Other people visited their grandparents for Christmas; we couldn't get to my grandparents' houses until Christmas afternoon, after a flight on a virtually empty airplane early Christmas morning. In the first eight years of my life I went to three churches every Sunday because my dad served a three-point parish.

I lived and breathed church, even in the secular Pacific Northwest. We lived church so much that the only time we could stay home from church was when one of us was sick. Our options on a sick day were to listen to the radio broadcast of First Presbyterian Church of Seattle or to hold our own service at home with Scripture readings and singing hymns. Even when my dad was on vacation, we went to a different church.

But we were not the Christians who prayed around the flag-pole. God cares about countries the way God cares about sports, I thought: not on anyone's side, just deeply loving of all creation. I decided certain things about those kids who would pray around a flagpole, based not in small part on my own experiences of several of them in the classroom and in peer groups. They believed that the United States is a Christian nation, belying increasing religious diversity and the constitutional principle of freedom of religion. They glorified one country over another through prayer. They were uptight, holier-than-thou, prudish, antievolution kids who prayed for a country whose creation lay in war and invasion.

My parents taught me to be the kind of Christian who believed that men and women were equal, that evolution and Christian faith were not incompatible, that we should be upset about the ways in which a full life were denied to people because of their class, race, religion, country of origin. My mother marched in Seattle's gay pride parade with her parishioners. We participated in boycotts and supported the Southern Poverty Law Center. I was indignant about injustice by the time I entered high school, and I had plenty of theological and biblical resources at my fingertips to back up my indignation.

The more I was able to choose my friends, the less willing I was to engage with people I thought would be the type to pray around the flagpole. By the time I went to seminary, I decided that I didn't want to engage conservatives anymore. I was friends with agnostics and religiously unaffiliated people who had liberal tendencies before I was friends with anyone I deemed a conservative. Pentecostals, evangelicals, fundamentalists, and conservative mainliners blended together in my head.

Those definitions and divisions didn't last. In seminary I sat across a table with my Introduction to Theology classmate, a Pentecostal minister at Chicago's Apostolic Church of God, and we discussed our theological convictions around evil. She said that she believed in the devil. I said I didn't believe in the personification of evil. We agreed that evil showed up in interactions, systems, and structures. Through many of my (very patient) classmates, I found that social liberalism could be paired with theological conservatism. Dynamics of race, class, and region upset the categories that

I had defined by observing white middle-income Christians in the Pacific Northwest.

These challenges to the definitions that I used to shape my social and religious life disrupted my rigid understanding of who was part of my family. I got to know Baptists, Pentecostals, and Lutherans who reminded me that we Christians are not so different. For all my anticonservative sentiment, I could be quite conservative myself. And Christians whom I used to avoid because I decided that they were judgmental could be the epitome of gracious hospitality, pointing out my own tendencies to judge and dismiss entire groups of people without even getting to know them. I discovered that I did not dislike multiple ways of reading and interpreting Scripture, nor did it really hurt me to sit in disagreement. In fact, my expressions of faith deepened in the midst of all that difference.

Perhaps we are meant to be together after all. I could learn from those Christians who pray around the flagpole.

The Challenge

Ecumenism is the practice of Christian unity across churches and communions (which some call denominations), with "practice" being the operative word. The challenge to ecumenism in the twenty-first century begins with the joy and annoyance of diversity. My generation of Christian leaders has been conditioned to see diversity as a gift, but in fact it creates a lot of work. We Christians have been engaged in passive-aggressive conflict, avoidance, and all-out brawls over our differences since before the church really began. Want to get a biblical perspective on ecumenism? Check out some Pauline and Deutero-Pauline letters. Take a look at the Gospels, and get a glimpse into the conflicts within Judaism at the beginning of the Common Era, and you'll see that we Christians come by this honestly.

Follow that through the split between the East and the West over the doctrine of the Trinity, through issues around indulgences and abuses by church officials, until you come to arguments over baptism, and keep going to today. In the United States we are all welcome to worship as Christians, and we have a dizzying array of options. Focused on the end times? There are churches for that.

Focused on doing good in a world of hurt? There are churches for that. Determined to follow what the Bible says? Choose the verse you're pulling out of context: there are churches for all kinds of ways to follow biblical mandates based upon what they read into these verses.

The mid-twentieth century saw the creation of councils of churches. Thanks to this robust movement, we as Christians have formal channels through which to practice work, prayer, worship, and witness together across splits of doctrine and tradition. These official bodies—international, national, regional, local—provide infrastructure for conversation, doing theology, engaging in peace and justice work, and responding to a community in crisis.

I began to participate in ecumenical work as an individual and as a representative of a communion in the late 1990s. My colleagues, who had been in the work much longer than I had, spoke longingly of the heyday of ecumenism. This heyday seemed to have over-lapped with the years in which the mainline churches in the United States held much more social power and dominance. There was real hope for the Council on Christian Unity to bring communions much closer together. Ecumenical councils had plenty of money. Justice work was alive and well at all levels. Twentieth-century ecu-menism did not include many of the most exciting global Christian movements, but it did provide structures to meet across difference, particularly when denominationalism was much stronger. It provided structures to address "isms" and to give religious leaders op-portunities to learn from each other. This ecumenism brought us some pretty great holiday bazaars and cooperative special services. This ecumenism provides the structure necessary for when great tragedy strikes the country or the local community.

To be sure, this ecumenism is largely structural, and it does not consistently require that we as Christians participate relationally at the grassroots level. It does not include many evangelical and Pentecostal churches and traditions, although international struc-tures have established formal dialogues and working groups with Pentecostals and Roman Catholics. And these formal structures are elite. Participation in councils of churches is hard to access at the national and international level.

It should be noted that the work of international councils of churches, whether it be the World Council of Churches or the World

Communion of Reformed Churches, continues to be vibrant and important. Nowhere else are there such sustained conversations between councils and representatives from diverse traditions. The World Council of Churches is a space in which much work toward justice and human rights takes place. But in the United States most people and churches are relatively isolated from the international community. In my travels I have noticed how citizens of other countries seem so connected to international governance and politics, in contrast to the ignorance of Americans to international affairs. Ecumenism in the United States is often isolated from the good and important work taking place internationally.

Beyond councils of churches are the multiple conversations held between two communions, or multiple. The Presbyterian Church (USA) holds ongoing bilateral conversations with the Holy See. The Formula of Agreement[1] is the result of multilateral talks between the Presbyterian Church (USA), the United Church of Christ, the Evangelical Lutheran Church in America, and the Reformed Church in America. The Evangelical Lutheran Church in America is in full communion with the Episcopal Church and the Moravian Church.

The challenge of ecumenism is that it isn't over. The way we have done it for years is no longer as central to the landscape. Where the mid-twentieth century saw the controversial creation of councils of churches, the early twenty-first century is seeing the creation of networks of individual congregational leaders, existing alongside councils of churches. Boundaries of language, theological tradition, race, and class have kept Christians separate, and now boundaries relating to the affirmation of women's leadership, the place of GLBT (gay, lesbian, bisexual, transgender) and queer people in Christian life, and the extent to which engagement in political discourse is acceptable are maintaining new separations. Ideologies separate Christians as much as denominations used to define groups of believers.

New ecumenical conversations have emerged. The World Council of Churches does not include Pentecostal traditions, but this structure and others engage in formal dialogues with Pentecostals. These national and international conversations followed the work done at the local level among diverse Christians. One conversation revolves around whether or not a minister in one tradition can be accepted into leadership in another. It is a very different conversation that happens when churches join together to work for the healing of a community that experiences a crisis, such as a massive tornado or gun violence.

There is another layer to this work. While churches and religious leaders grapple with doctrinal differences, Christians every day navigate work and life with diverse people. While churches engage in complicated quarrels that began centuries ago, Christians face the reality of needing to gain fluency in interreligious dialogue. We are confronted with multi-faith families, neighbors who practice another religion, and the growing population of nonaffiliated. Sometimes interreligious dialogue is a little easier for us. It can be easier to work as a congregation on an interfaith build of a house for low-income people than it is to cross the mainline-Pentecostal divide, for instance. But interreligious work will remain a challenge in part because our own house is such a mess. One Christian group proclaims love and acceptance for gay and lesbian people, while another proclaims that God hates homosexuals.

Into the midst of such diversity and disagreement enters a twenty-first-century ecumenism. This ecumenism moves beyond holiday bazaars and midday midweek Thanksgiving services among mostly mono-racial groups of believers to a messy, problematic, broad-ranging ecumenism grappling with being Christian community in the midst of the lived realities of all believers. We need a redefined ecumenism with relevant structures, an ecumenism that pushes us to be gracious instead of polarized, genuine instead of polite. We need a more inclusive and genuine relationship among traditions, among clergy, among laity, both within formal structures and through new ways of being.

Now is the time to make ecumenism stretchy. Instead of abandoning the council of churches model and the top-level bilateral conversations model, we need to reach between ways of doing, so ecumenism for the early twenty-first century looks like a mad, beautiful mix of what used to be and what is emerging. Councils of churches have a ways to go before they crumble. Formal structures are necessary. We think that we don't need them until we do. The Formula of Agreement doesn't seem like a big deal, until a leader is called to a position in another church. Councils of churches have real impact, real meaning, and build real relationships. The World

Council of Churches' efforts with churches calling on the International Monetary Fund to cancel Haiti's debt in the aftermath of the massive 2010 earthquake were successful. Without formal structures, we might not be forced to interact with different traditions or be able to effect change at the international policy level. It is easy enough for a United Methodist church to hold a joint Thanksgiving worship service with the local Congregationalists, but to engage with the Greek Orthodox community down the street may require a formal structure to help shape the conversation. The best way to engage with other communions as a newly arrived religious leader is to connect with a local council of churches.

If we as Christians rely only on the formal structures, however, we will find that there are limits to the Christians with whom we relate. If we rely only on relationships, we will find that there are limits to that approach. A new, "stretchy" ecumenism reaches between modern and postmodern religious structures in the United States. Being "stretchy" means practicing ecumenism in all the ways that are effective, including councils of churches, top-level bilateral conversations, as well as local efforts between neighboring churches or national networks of local church leaders from diverse church backgrounds, drawn together by a common passion for mission. Being "stretchy" means also starting with just a cup of tea between a Spanish-speaking Methodist and an English-speaking evangelical. It means we are each called to stretch between what is simultaneously known, comfortable, awkward, intimidating, and difficult.

Why Does It Matter?

"Where two or more are gathered in my name, I'm there with them," said Jesus (Matthew 18:20 CEB). Gathering across difference? Well, "if food causes the downfall of my brother or sister, I won't eat meat ever again" (1 Corinthians 8:13 CEB). "It's a good thing not to eat meat or drink wine or to do anything that trips your brother or sister" (Romans 14:21 CEB), because we as Christians will be in relationship with those who are different from one another. Different cultures and expectations come together to worship, and we are guided to be attentive to how our behavior contributes to the larger community. Christian unity is for real, according to what we know of our Christian story from these verses. After all, we are pretty much playing for the same team in the end.

Too often, Christian unity is confused with uniformity. Unity brings to mind sober, serious conversations among male clerics dressed in robes, discussing how to respond to the latest set of differences regarding the Eucharist. Anyone who has practiced ecumenism knows that unity is not boring. Unity is exciting because it requires that we be real with each other about our differences. In order to come to a common place, we have to work through the very real disagreements that we have. Everyone in that place looks different, speaks differently, has a different home life, eats different foods, but comes together to agree on what really matters.

I went to India for a consultation with the World Council of Churches when I was twenty-one. I thought that I had known ecumenism through the local United Ministries of Higher Education group, local bazaars, and community-wide vacation Bible schools. This consultation on women and racism changed everything. Here was a group of women from different countries, some from churches I had never heard of, gathering to talk about a dizzying array of local, national, and international manifestations of gender and racial oppression. We had difficulty settling on one definition. The structure of the organization that convened us was modern: each woman came from a member church of the World Council of Churches. Our work was postmodern: multiple realities coexisted at the same time. We had different concerns and affiliations, even disagreeing with one another. An American woman talked about the importance of Title IX and the importance of gender-specific sports clothing allowing for freedom of movement; Indian women then commiserated with one another about the reduced numbers of Indian girls wearing traditional clothing. What was important to the Indian women were the ways in which India was being made to look like Europe and the United States, causing a loss of culture. What was important to the American woman was that girls be able to participate fully in sports. What mattered to both, however, was the impact of racism on girls and women everywhere.

I had known the realities of racial segregation growing up and through college, but when I moved to Chicago, I realized that the reason why urban sociologists have a tendency to study Chicago is that the city is an extreme example. My professor wasn't lying when he said that a street acts like a line to separate one neighborhood from another. A street in Chicago means everything: class distinctions, race and culture distinctions, differences in access, social circles, and church circles. Churches, with a few exceptions, remain segregated, and so do denominations. Lutherans, Episcopalians, Presbyterians, and Unitarians remain overwhelmingly white denominations (with small and strong contingents of faithful people of color). Historically black denominations remain so. Sometimes the challenge of real ecumenism is the challenge of racism and classism. I have known some racially specific churches with higher class status (often in the suburbs) to partner with racially specific churches with lower class status (often in urban centers), but it is perhaps not altogether common for a member of a liberal urban Congregational storefront church to walk next door to the African American Baptist church and strike up a conversation. Ecumenism is a great opportunity for churches to begin to challenge these social conventions, and it has been for decades.

Black and white churches, some of them gay-friendly, partner to provide meals and shelter for homeless people during the winter, and they provide transportation to families of the incarcerated to prisons on weekends for visits. A largely Puerto Rican congregation in a working-class suburb partnered with a largely Korean congregation down the street. Together they held youth events, and they found the experiences of immigration and generational challenges among families to be common to both communities. This is the relatively mundane work that brings together different Christians to do work that matters and allows for real conversations.

Christian unity requires a stretchy ecumenism whereby multiple realities are allowed to exist. If Christ is among us wherever we are gathered, we are bound to one another in the midst of our disagreements about who can take Communion and who is eligible to say the words of institution. When we return to our home communities, these experiences make us contemplate how our own actions and behaviors would be received by Christians in other places and traditions. We may be more careful as a result. The reality of ecumenism in the twenty-first century goes beyond pragmatism to a struggle to be both true and accountable. If God is present when we are gathered, how do we build on that presence when we are apart?

Questions

What would it be like to engage in ecumenism with Christians whose faith is significantly different from our own? Ecumenical relations can feel like a tourist experience. We decide on a destination church or hear of an event that we want to attend. We look up directions and travel times to the location. Upon our arrival, the things that make an impression on us are the external manifestations and habits of the faith of that church: the sights, sounds, and smells of worship stick in our minds. The words that they use that are different from the ones we use. We find aspects of the experience that match our home experiences. Something will look familiar.

I love being a tourist. I have been a tourist in Baptist, Pentecostal, nondenominational, Lutheran, Episcopal/Anglican, Methodist, Disciples, Roman Catholic, and Congregational church settings in the United States. I have been a tourist at United Church of Canada events, Mar Thoma church services in India, and Presbyterian services in South Korea, Guatemala, and Egypt. I have attended worship services in Vietnamese, Korean, Arabic, and Spanish. This is something that I enjoy, and this is also what we might call an "occupational hazard" for a minister.

The problem with the tourist experience is that there is often no accountability between the visitor and the church. Real, stretchy ecumenism is grounded in relationship. Relationships take work, and they also have the potential to transform each one of us. I have come to dislike mainline liberal mockery of churches in which worshipers speak in tongues, because the relationships that I have with Christians in whose churches this is a regular practice have grounded an unfamiliar spiritual gift in a relationship that I am unwilling to trivialize. Ideally, coming back to shared worship spaces will change from feeling like tourist experiences into more closely resembling worshipful gatherings even in the midst of difference.

How might we as Christians engage across contentious difference? We as Christians have genuine disagreements with one another. We have real differences of belief and practice. We are set in our ways. Infant baptism? How can a one-year-old claim her or his own belief in Jesus Christ? Speaking in tongues? Is that for real? Working to end the death penalty? What business does a church have messing in the political process, when churches are supposed to attend to spiritual matters? Supporting the invasion of (insert name of country here)? What kind of church supports an invasion of a sovereign nation and the deaths of its citizens and of the invading nation's military personnel? How can I be genuine with those so different from myself, instead of just polite?

How can we bridge the gaps between international ecumenical work and the lives of local congregations? How is it that the local worshiping community may make the work of top-level ecumenical structures, programs, and activism real? It is particularly complex when religious leaders are already supposed to keep up with local happenings, the policies and trends in their own denominations, emerging youth ministry techniques, and the latest scholarship on leadership and biblical studies, as well as interreligious work, when information about international ecumenical work is distributed unevenly in North American religious circles. Often the only times in the lives of worshiping communities that global Christianity is made real are when missionaries visit, churches go on short-term mission trips, or during a celebration of World Communion Sunday. What is an overworked, undercompensated religious leader to do?

Practices

We often talk past each other, using different syntax, with different definitions. To make our ecumenism real and stretchy, we need to practice a few things. The first is to practice learning our own traditions and to become literate in one's own tradition. Ecumenical and interreligious conversations help us to deepen our own beliefs and can be very clarifying. Being able to articulate what it is we believe and why we believe it will go a long way toward making ecumenical work and conversation fruitful. Most of us are not rigid adherents to everything we were taught, and we may learn that there is more variation among some groups than we imagined.

The second practice is learning how to have conversations. Real conversation can be very taxing, particularly across deep divides of race, class, biblical interpretive lenses, spiritual convictions, and conceptions of what it means to act like a Christian. It is one thing to build a house or feed the hungry together, but engaging in conversations about baptism, how churches are impacted by the socioeconomic makeup of communities segregated by race and class, the role of women in the church, or the place of gay and lesbian people in ministry—this is what makes ecumenism far more complicated. Essential equipping for ministry and Christian witness for all believers is having the capacity to engage in genuine conversation without becoming combative or defensive.

The third practice is about language. It can help to learn how to code-switch; the language that we use in our own communities might need to be different from the language that we use to speak with others in other communities. Code-switching is not about being insincere but rather about how to best represent ourselves while communicating effectively with others. As the leader of a community, or as a member of a community, think about becoming literate not only in your own tradition but also in the vocabulary of multiple Christian traditions. You say "General Synod," I say "Annual Conference." You say "Eucharist," I say "Communion." You say "District Superintendent," I say "Executive Presbyter." You say "converted," I say "confirmed." You say "believer's baptism," I say "infant baptism." You say "Bible-based," I say "grounded in Scripture." Ongoing interaction and encounter will strengthen the graciousness of our syntax.

All this aside, the fourth practice is a dogged, determined, gracious presence. Showing up is number one. Walk down the street to another religious group's gathering place, knock on the door, and have a conversation. Build a relationship. Be honest about your differences. Ask for explanations, and offer your own when it is helpful. Be present to that community when it is important, even when it is inconvenient or uncomfortable. Done by religious leaders, this is an important step. Done by whole religious communities, this is a revolution.

In seminary many of us interact with people who are significantly theologically different from ourselves. We have to interact because our grades hinge on that interaction, but the gift of having to talk, pray, worship, and work with one another is that we can emerge with meaningful relationships. Members of congregations interact with diverse Christians at work and school every day, but they are not always given the opportunity to engage or question the person who worships or believes differently. What if church were an invitation to do just that?

I know what assuming does to you and me, but here are some practical assumptions to make in the midst of this stretchy ecumenism:

- Assume that you don't know everything.
- Assume that other worship styles, spiritual expressions, theologies, beliefs, and practices are equally valid expressions of Christianity.
- Assume that being ecumenical sometimes means doing extra work.
- Assume that your community needs you to be ecumenical in new ways for the sake of the neighborhood, the city, the state, the country.
- Assume that members of the congregation may be as well-equipped, if not better-equipped, than the leaders of the congregation to engage in ecumenical ventures.

A Baptist, a Presbyterian, and a Pentecostal walk into a classroom together. Or a homeless shelter. Or a church. Or a state government building. Or the United Nations. It's not the beginning of a joke. It's the expression of a commitment to the witness of the gospel.

Questions for Consideration

1. Do you and your congregation prefer to interact with certain churches over others, or certain kinds of Christians over others? Why is that?
2. How do you engage with people or churches with whom you have significant disagreements? How are you gracious to one another in the midst of it?
3. What new ecumenical relationships might you explore in your neighborhood? Your city or town? Your region?

Note

1. The Formula of Agreement began in 1997 between four communions, having found doctrinal consensus. The practical result is that churches from these communions may worship together and exchange ministers.

Part III

Reinventing Justice

8

changing CHURCH TALK

JESSICA VAZQUEZ TORRES

I STILL REMEMBER THE DAY I LOST MY LANGUAGE. I WAS SITTING IN a classroom at Lyman High School in Longwood, Florida, watching my classmates and teacher, hearing them pronounce words and express thoughts but understanding nothing. I failed to understand English and lacked the experience and context to understand the cultural cues that would have helped make sense of what was taking place in our conversation. My brain struggled for an entire academic year to learn not just vocabulary but also rules of grammar, facial expressions, idioms, and how bodies moved in English. For the next year of my life I would utter no words in English to anyone in my school.

I found language again. However, the way there was difficult. I had to retrain my brain to think in English, my body to mold itself into ways of communicating that fit the contours of English, my tongue to enunciate new combinations of letters and utter new sounds, and my imagination to compose with an economy and precision of words that was foreign to the Spanish lexicon and grammar patterns that I was molded into from birth. As my command of the English language increased, my relationship to my mother tongue shifted. Its primacy over my thought process decreased as I abandoned its romantic tonality for the precision and sharpness of academic English. No longer did Spanish roll off my tongue, invade my dreams, or take over my body.

As my body transitioned from Spanish to English, so did the language of my faith. I grew up a mainline Christian influenced by the puritanical and evangelistic language and practices passed down from missionaries to their folks of Puerto Rican converts. My language of faith was gendered and embodied. God was male and father. Jesus was male and incarnate. Evil was personified. Demons were real. The Spirit was heard and seen, as it possessed the bodies of church attendees. Dreams were prophetic, and visions were retold in congregational spaces where their meaning was explored and at times debated. Faith, church, and religion were viscerally experienced.

I began my theological training and shaping filled with gendered, classed, and raced language and images of God. Four years in a progressive seminary transformed my faith language. God became gender neutral. Evil no longer resided in the devil but in sociocultural systems. Prophecy was declared suspect. Prophetic language was judiciously and seldom used. Critical thinking and the search for understanding mediated faith, evil, and the experience of the Spirit. At twenty-five, I found myself an ordained minister trapped between languages. The embodied, classed, and gendered language of faith that resided in the very sinews of my being and the disembodied intellectual language of theological education, which opened me up to think about the content of my faith, warred within me.

While I, in theory, value and affirm the impetus to extricate Christian language from gendered, classed, and raced boxes that reinforce dominant cultural norms and experiences as definitive of American Christianity, I also find meaning and comfort in the embodied nature of the gendered and often raced language that dominated my faith formation. Seminary left me little room to explore how all of these ways of speaking about God and the work of giving witness to God's grace, mercy, and justice could be compatible and simultaneously challenging. Entangled by the pernicious dichotomies so defining of United States dominant culture, I left seminary unable to see a linguistic way forward, and thus I replayed the linguistic tendencies that my theological education taught me. My aim became not to offend or ruffle any feathers. In the process, I ceased to speak in ways that were authentic, meaningful, or relevant either to the immigrant community that shaped me or to the dominant white Christian community that embraced me.

The Challenge

A dominant culture operates in the United States, setting the standards by which the country's citizens, residents, and institutions define what is considered normal, acceptable, and/or standard. By extension, it also defines what is not. I do not want to imply that the United States has a homogenous culture, because it does not. I do, however, assert that the dominant culture of this nation informs, shapes, and legitimates (or not) all cultural manifestations observed in this nation. The dominant culture of the United States is Christian, hegemonic, capitalist, militaristic, individualistic, homophobic, transphobic, sexist, heterosexist, xenophobic, racist, classist, ageist, and obsessed with youth, beauty, individual heroes, and personal freedom. Few in the United States will claim it as their culture, but this culture shapes every citizen and resident of this nation.

In this cultural context a particular iteration of Christian language, a more conservative form, is at the center of much sociopolitical debate, while another, more progressive/liberal form is relegated to the margins of our national conversation. Centered faith language is, by and large, punitive, sexist, homophobic, xenophobic, militaristic, consumeristic, and shrouded in patriotic devotion. It is language concerned almost exclusively with legislating individual moral conduct while giving credence to collective and systemic actions such as war, which destroy life. Social reaction to this linguistic violence is often to reject most Christian faith language as irrelevant, disconnected from the reality of the world we live in, and anachronistic.

One of the most pressing challenges facing American Christianity today is the hijacking of Christian language by conservative Christians and the reactionary divestment from progressive/liberal Christian spheres of recognizable Christian language. Conservatives have effectively claimed dominance over Christian language and semantics. To say that one is Christian in the United States often results in automatically being linked with particular social policies, political ideologies, and value frameworks concerned with the preservation of a true American way of life, the resurrection of evangelistic crusades for the soul of the nation, and the elimination of other religious expressions. Amidst this appropriation of conservative Christian language, a distinctively progressive Christian voice committed to speak against sociosystemic forms of oppression and marginalization, Christian hegemony, United States warmongering, and corporate abuse has lost ground.

Christians seeking to advance the gospel's call to shalom, and to live out a commitment to social justice, have been so afraid to appear complicit with this form of Christian language that they have often given up use of words, phrases, images, concepts, and traditions. While this divestment is taking place among progressive Christian communities, ideologically right-wing and conservative Christians bombard the American viewing and listening audiences daily with misappropriated Christian language, images, and theological ideas. Everything from the classic claim that the United States is an "exceptional" nation blessed by God, to the Fox News host of conspiracy theories regarding the war against Christianity being waged by everyone who is "liberal," Muslim, secular, atheist, and/or agnostic. Even Pope Francis's *Evangelii Gaudium* ("The Joy of the Gospel") has been dismissed by powerful spokespersons from the Christian conservative camp as an erroneous, naïve, and misguided justification of socialism.[1] Caught in the middle between "liberal" distancing from overtly Christian language and "conservative" claims of exclusivity regarding Christian language and semantics are the 70 percent of American adults who consider themselves Christian.[2] While some of these men and women live comfortably at the extremes of conservative and liberal, the data suggest among young people ages 18 to 33 "a stability among religious moderates and decreased appeal in religious conservatism."[3] I would argue that many, if not most young people, desire a faith that is theologically relevant and that speaks to the political and economic challenges being faced in ways which demand social change.

Often those of us on the progressive end of American Christianity avoid religious language altogether, adopting sociopolitical language and frameworks instead to make our claims about the message of the gospel. We hide behind our intellectualism and reason, offering harsh critiques of the emotional and embodied expressions of faith that we see among our more evangelical siblings while secretly envying their freedom. We fear the accusation that we might be acting in evangelistic ways. We hold on to superficial practices such as "WWJD" in order to avoid the hard work of critiquing the

United States's manifestation of the faith that we claim and our exercise of it.

The progressive and liberal elements of American Christianity have been advocating for the adoption of colorblind and gender-neutral language for decades, and I would argue that this push to divest the language of Christianity of its corporeal and erotic reality while seeking to liberate has also backfired. The result of this endeavor in language transformation has not been social inclusion for those socially marginalized and oppressed, but instead forms of political correctness masking the myriad ways in which progressive/liberal American Christianity fails to critique how church institutions, culture, theology, biblical interpretation, and practices leave social ills unaddressed or address them superficially. Furthermore, I would argue that in pushing so hard against gendered, classed, and raced ways of expressing faith, those of us in the progressive/liberal realm of Christianity have created spaces that prevent genuine struggle with the limitations of our faith claims, as we are too concerned with correcting the "linguistic" sexism, racism, heterosexism, and ableism (to name just a few) of those with whom we differ. We have become stuck in words instead of striving to hear each other past the limitations of language in ways that enable us to focus on the systemic dynamics that perpetuate oppression with appropriated "faith-speak."

My Big Idea

Robert Kegan and Lisa Laskow Lahey, of the Harvard Graduate School of Education, observe, "The forms of speaking we have available to us regulate the forms of thinking, feeling, and meaning making to which we have access, which in turn constrain how we see the world and act in it."[4] In other words, the language that we use has the power to nurture in us a spirit of openness or to close us off, to cultivate and expand our imagination or to stifle it, to influence and thus shape worldview and action. Language matters not simply because it enables a variety of forms of communication, but because it limits or expands our ability to consider what it means to be a Christian in the world and to struggle with the implications of enacting one's faith in meaningful and relevant ways linked to it.

Consider the following anecdote. I once worked for and with a mainline Protestant denomination as they searched for ways to challenge systemic racism in their church structure and regenerate a commitment among its members toward the elimination of racism from their structures. In my travels throughout the church I often heard liberal folks say something like, "If we're going to be a fully welcoming and progressive church, we must teach the new immigrants joining our denomination how to be *really* one of us." I never ceased to be taken aback by this sentiment, as its implication was that most of the people joining the denomination were not "real Christians" like "us," and if we could teach them, our internal issues with sexism and heterosexism would disappear. For me, the power of this often-used phrase resided in the pronoun "we" and the adjective "real." Who is the "we" being assumed? What determines what makes a person or a community a member of the "we"? Is there a test to be a part of the "we"? Furthermore, what does it mean to be "really" anything? What are the markers of the "real"? Who are the determiners of what and who is "real"?

Similarly, when I met with more conservative leaders of the denomination (particularly those located within immigrant and people of color communities), they would explain their resistance to antiracism work by saying something like, "'Antiracism' is a code word for 'welcoming homosexuals' to the church, and we refuse to have the denomination impose its liberal politics on us." As a queer Latina, I was challenged by these expressions, and yet given the liberal push to "make them like us," I understood somewhat the conservative frustration. I wanted to ask these men and women struggling for authentic recognition, access, and power within a historically white denomination how they could separate their struggle for self-determination from that of other groups within the community. What was so threatening about addressing the links between heterosexism, homophobia, and racism? Were they upset about the links or about the notion of imposition?

As I went about the work of engaging people in efforts against systemic racism, I found myself caught in and by the differing ways various communities within one denomination defined and interpreted the call to reconciliation. I was struck by the intractability of their claims about the call to reconciliation, and their unwillingness to enter into honest dialogue. Each community believed that they held the truth and spoke with such certainty that all room for mutual learning and dialogue became impossible. Observing from the sidelines and leaving in droves were Christians, new and old, fed up with feuds that keep the church focused on inward struggles instead of giving witness to God's justice, love, and grace.

It behooves Christians to reexamine the language that we use in communicating the gospel's message, investigate how our interpretations of sacred texts might be closing us off to hearing other interpretations, and inquire what language and which interpretations must be abandoned, which ones must be reclaimed, and what must be created anew if the faith we profess is to remain a relevant voice in the United States and, by extension, the world. It is my big idea that unshackling Christian language from liberalism's colorblind and gender-neutral political correctness will create the linguistic space for social justice seeking, prophetic, and radically loving American Christianity to find more effective ways to speak in and to the present cultural context, which is starving for a faith story that challenges the dominant narrative of hegemonic Christianity on the one hand and individualistic spiritualities on the other.

My big idea emerges from my experiences as a liberal/progressive mainline Protestant Christian frustrated by the inability of many progressive Christians to relate to, engage in fruitful conversation with, and hear the critique that our conservative brothers and sisters may offer us, our faith expression, and our culture. It is informed also by my own experiences in finding a language and semantic tools with which to engage my socially conservative Christian parents in a mutually respectful dialogue about my sexuality. Finally, it is also important to say that for me this unshackling of Christian language does not intend to advocate Christian linguistic relativism or to abandon all the gains that the moves toward inclusive language have brought us. Instead, I seek to explore "both/and" ways of approaching faith language so that we may create a space where we can question the impact of our speech without policing the words that we use to communicate.

Case Study: The Language of Racial Reconciliation

The need for linguistic liberation is seen compellingly in the way most Protestant Christian communities in the United States approach their communal conversations about racism, racial inequality, and white supremacy. It is important to recognize that the Protestant

Christian church in the United States is not unique in its lack of effectiveness around these issues. Like all American institutions, the church's efforts to address the social evils of race and racism are hampered by the profound individualism of the United States, by a conceptualization of sin as something that pertains only to individual behavior or morality, by the notion that the United States is a nation where historic social ills have no bearing in the present, by a misguided belief that legal changes in the middle of the twentieth century eliminated racism from our culture and institutions, and by a collective inability to think critically about the ways individual human beings are caught in self-perpetuating systems of oppression.

Given these social and cultural dynamics, mainline Protestant Christians in the United States often approach conversations about race, racism, and racial reconciliation with at least four problematic assumptions: (1) racism is most often perpetuated by ignorant individuals who must be educated to overcome their bigotry; (2) racism is exclusively a spiritual issue, and in order to achieve racial reconciliation individual racists must transform their hearts and minds; (3) racism manifests itself almost exclusively at the interpersonal level, which results in approaches to addressing racism that revolve around relationship healing and building; (4) racism operates in isolation from other social evils as opposed to operating in co-constitutive ways with other forms of social marginalization such as classism and sexism. These assumptions and the sociocultural context that produces them generate a way of thinking and talking about racial reconciliation that resists naming the historical dynamics that have created sociocultural systems that perpetuate the domination of people of color in order to protect and preserve the comfort and power of white society in the United States.

Rare is the congregation where conversations about racial reconciliation permeate the preaching and religious education year-round. All too common is the segregation of conversations about racial reconciliation and the struggle against racism to a few weeks in February during African American history month. This of course has the unfortunate consequence of locking conversations about race, racism, and racial reconciliation into a "black and white" binary box and spreading the fallacy that racism only affects African Americans in the United States, which in turn obfuscates both the ways other communities of color experience racism and how white society is both harmed and privileged by systemic racism.

Consequently, conversations about racial reconciliation within many mainline Protestant Christian communities are often marked by a desperate politeness that keeps the dialogue superficial. The racial reconciliation approaches at work in many mainline Protestant Christian communities in the United States prioritize getting along over challenging structures of power that privilege some at the expense of many; embrace tolerance over inclusion; and settle for politeness over substantive relationships across racial lines. In these approaches the absence of outright racial conflict is seen as the goal even if systemic forms of discrimination remain unchallenged.

The struggle for racial reconciliation within the Christian community is further impaired by the fallacy of colorblindness, which maintains that the most effective way to end racism is to simply cease to see, acknowledge, and speak about racial differences. The ideology of colorblindness prevents its adherents from naming the reality of race and privilege in the United States. It causes communities seeking racial justice to operate under the assumption that the United States is a society in which all human beings are seen and treated equally. Since acknowledging racial differences is to be racist, colorblindness can render a community silent in the face of systemic racial injustice. The consequence is calls for racial reconciliation that are cheap and shallow, ones that often fail to acknowledge all of the ways in which the church maintains and validates the culture and ideologies that maintain racism in place.

But what if the conversation about race, racism, racial reconciliation, and racial justice within the faith community were unshackled? How might conversations about racism shift if people of faith were equipped with analytical skills to assess the dynamics of power at work in the maintenance of social injustice? What might change if the approaches to racial reconciliation within mainline Protestant Christian churches invited people to think of racism in a multiplicity of ways: as individual sin, as structural evil, and as a cultural malaise? What would happen if congregations were equipped to talk about racism not simply as a phenomenon concerning African American and white people in the United States exclusively?

Grounding in Tradition and Scripture

Effective racial reconciliation work is grounded in the Gospels and informed by the tradition of the church community, and it is undertaken as a spiritual discipline. I write as one claiming space in the Reformed tradition. We come together under our motto, *Ecclesia reformata, semper reformanda,* which means "The church reformed is always to be reforming." Presbyterian theologian Anna Case-Winters reflects upon the meaning of this founding principle:

> *Ecclesia reformata, semper reformanda.* This motto calls us to something more radical than we have imagined. It challenges both liberal and conservative impulses and the habits and agendas we have lately fallen into. It brings a prophetic critique to our cultural accommodation—either to the past or to the present—and calls us to communal and institutional repentance. It invites us, as people who worship and serve a living God, to be open to being "re-formed" according to the Word of God and the call of the Spirit.[5]

To claim any part of the reformed faith is to be comfortable with dilemma, committed to dialogue, and willing to engage in debate with civility and humility so that the church might be transformed.[6] Openness to being "re-formed" becomes key in efforts to unshackle the language of the progressive faith community, for it creates a space to interrogate tradition, interpretations of the gospel message, communal practices, and the very institution of the church. Tradition and communal practice matter because these ground our movement in the world with affirmations like this one from the Brief Statement of Faith of the Presbyterian Church (USA):

> *In a broken and fearful world*
> *the Spirit gives us courage*
> *to pray without ceasing,*
> *to witness among all peoples to Christ as Lord and Savior,*
> *to unmask idolatries in Church and culture,*
> *to hear the voices of peoples long silenced,*
> *and to work with others for justice, freedom, and peace.*

Christianity is a faith built upon the claim that the creator God became incarnate in one named "Jesus," who for a brief period in his life challenged the structures of his society, creating spaces where all could experience life restored. Walter Brueggemann, reflecting upon the ministry of Jesus, writes, "In both his preaching and his very presence Jesus of Nazareth presented the ultimate criticism of the royal consciousness. He has, in fact, dismantled and nullified its claims."[7] Think of the stories of the woman with the hemorrhage, the Samaritan woman at the well, and the man with the withered hand; in all of these Jesus is challenging dominant culture practices that perpetuated social marginalization. Think of Jesus' teachings outside of the synagogue, in the plain and on the mount, and around the Sea of Galilee; these reveal a pattern of proclamation that challenges the power structure of the time by announcing a new order.

We live in an increasingly polarized society. Racial and class segregation are on the rise. Educational and economic gaps widen the chasm between the "haves" and "have-nots." Poverty is accepted as inevitable and as the result of people lacking ambition. War is justified theologically as a necessary step to ensure the spread of free, democratic, and Christian society. Violence against the planet and all of its inhabitants is the cost of maintaining "our way" of life. The general secretary of the former World Alliance of Reformed Churches, Dr. Setri Nyomi, reflecting on what it means to live out faith in our challenging times, says, "Can Christians today be inspired to express a living faith which addresses the challenges of our days? What is called for is not easy answers, but the readiness to struggle with the resources which those who have gone before us have left as a legacy of living faith for their times."[8]

Can we inspire people to hope not by giving them simplistic and feel-good faith language that lulls the community into a sense of comfort? Can we awaken their imagination with words, rituals, and practices rooted in tradition but adapted to equip the people for the task of building the realm of God? Can our language move progressive people of faith to action? How might the proclamation and faith practice of the progressive faith commitment bring good news to the poor, release to the captives, recovery of sight to the blind, liberty to the oppressed, and announce the acceptable year of the Lord (Luke 4:18-19)?

Into the conundrum of life that baffles, words must be spoken and gestures given that will remind people of their ethical responsibilities toward each other. The progressive faith community must reclaim and liberate the gospel of Jesus Christ. The time has come to unleash the power of a living word upon a society in desperate need of meaning. Progressive people of faith must, invoking the work of Carter Heyward, save Jesus—and the Gospels that hold his teachings and those of his followers—from those who are right.[9]

Questions for Consideration

1. How might your faith community reclaim its language in order to address the great public missional[10] issues facing American society: hunger, poverty, war, greed, and racism (to name just a few)?

2. How might your community awaken the imagination of its members? What rituals and practices might have to be adapted to facilitate this process?

3. How might the proclamation and faith practice of the progressive faith commitment bring good news to the poor, release to the captives, recovery of sight to the blind, liberty to the oppressed, and announce the acceptable year of the Lord?

4. How might your church offer comfort to the discomforted and discomfort to the comfortable in ways that do not lead to paralysis, resentment, or guilt?

5. Can the language and church talk of your community move progressive people of faith to action?

Notes

1. "It's Sad How Wrong Pope Francis Is (Unless It's a Deliberate Mistranslation By Leftists)," *The Rush Limbaugh Show*, November 27, 2013
(http://www.rushlimbaugh.com/daily/2013/11/27/it_s_sad_how_wrong_pope_francis_is_unless_it_s_a_deliberate_mistranslation_by_leftists). Rush Limbaugh, whose radio show has fifteen million listeners, insinuated that unless "liberals" purposely mistranslated the pontiff's words, the pope is erroneously condemning capitalism while defending Marxism. Limbaugh implied that the content of the papal exhortation cannot be seen as an accurate interpretation of the gospel.
2. Frank Newport, "Seven in 10 Americans Are Very or Moderately Religious," *Gallup Politics*, December 4, 2012 (http://www.gallup.com/poll/159050/seven-americans-moderately-religious.aspx).

3. Jonathan Merritt, "The Rise of the Christian Left in America," *The Atlantic*, July 25, 2013 (http://www.theatlantic.com/politics/archive/2013/07/the-rise-of-the-christian-left-in-america/278086/).

4. Robert Kegan and Lisa Laskow Lahey, *How the Way We Talk Can Change the Way We Work: Seven Languages for Transformation* (San Francisco: Jossey-Bass, 2002), 7.

5. Presbyterian Church (USA), "What Do Presbyterians Believe about 'Ecclesia Reformata, Semper Reformanda'?" *Presbyterians Today*, October 14, 2010 (http://www.presbyterianmission.org/ministries/today/reformed/).

6. William E. Chapman and Martha S. Gilliss, *Distinctively Presbyterian* (Louisville: Witherspoon Press, 2006), ix–xix.

7. Walter Brueggemann, *The Prophetic Imagination* (Minneapolis: Fortress Press, 2001), 80–81.

8. Setri Nyomi, "Living Faith in a Challenging Era," *The Princeton Seminary Bulletin* 26, no. 1 (2005): 9–21. This lecture was delivered in 2005 at a symposium honoring the ministry and leadership of Princeton Seminary president Dr. Iain Torrance.

9. Carter Heyward, *Saving Jesus from Those Who Are Right: Rethinking What It Means to Be a Christian* (Minneapolis: Fortress Press, 1999).

10. For this language I am indebted to Walter Brueggemann, *Journey to the Common Good* (Louisville: Westminster John Knox Press, 2010).

9

believers UNCHAINED

Why Christians Must Abolish Prisons or Stop Preaching the Gospel

MADELINE McCLENNEY-SADLER

When it was evening on that day, the first day of the week, and the doors of the house where the disciples had met were locked for fear of the Jews, Jesus came and stood among them and said, "Peace be with you...as the Father sent me, so I am sending you."

(John 20:19, 21b NRSV)

Note to the Reader

THE STAKES ARE HIGH. LET THE READER KEEP AN OPEN MIND IN order to avoid the mental state known by psychologists as denial. Denial may be good for a limited time to soften the harsh reality of a loss or crisis that obliterates our sense of security. Security, however, is an illusion. It will always be an illusion. We are not secure. However, we know who holds the future, and that is enough. Come with me on a journey to discover what is happening right before our eyes. It will be well with our souls because we know that all power belongs to God (Psalm 62:11).

Believers Unchained

Why must Christians abolish prisons? We may approach this from several viewpoints. A christocentric viewpoint would look at Jesus' purpose-driven life as announced in Luke 4:18-19. Here Jesus announces that he came to liberate the oppressed and to release those who are held captive. Given Jesus' unapologetic preference for the deliverance of oppressed people and his love for guilty people, it would be counterintuitive for Christians to support the maintenance of the cage as a solution to our social problems.

We may approach this issue from a practical viewpoint. It is well-established in peer-reviewed journals of psychology and sociology that punishment does not work. It does not reduce crime. Furthermore, the punishment that we mete out is grossly unfair to minorities and poor people.[1]

Alternatively, we may make the case that the network of prisons around the nation targets and holds in cages one in nine black males between the ages of eighteen and thirty-four.[2] Often accepted as usual and customary, this is an infectious epidemic of black male oppression. If resources are being marshaled to aid the epidemic of autism, which one in eighty-eight children are born with it today, how much more should aid be flowing to the one in nine black males and to the one in seventeen black girls born in 2001 who will go to jail or prison?[3]

While each of these perspectives alone would be sufficient to make the case that prisons must be abolished, the case that should be most compelling is that the biblical laws found in the Pentateuch (first five books of the Bible) establish a system for social control, mercy, and retribution, and yet they never instruct the recipients of the tradition to build a prison. After five hundred to a thousand years of carefully copying and preserving Hebrew Scriptures, not one author or copier of biblical law added an instruction to build a prison to punish a Hebrew who sinned against a neighbor or against Yahweh.

Millions of Judeo-Christian citizens in the United States defend grace, mercy, second chances, redemption, brotherly and sisterly love, love of enemies, and repentance while at the same time defending and voting for people who will fund the continuation of the prison-industrial complex (PIC). The PIC is the driving force behind intentionally genocidal policies targeting black men and black families. Prisons must be abolished in our lifetime. The continued use of the criminal justice system to strangle the black community to death is an outrage. There is overwhelming evidence of rampant unlawful capture, sentencing, and punishment that provides a mountain of proof that Christians are ignoring another holocaust of epic proportions.

If we have ever wondered why so many God-fearing people managed to hide their heads in the sand while our Jewish brothers and sisters were being rounded up and thrown into Nazi prisons for minor "offenses," we have only to look at genocide in the United States.

Part of the United Nations's definition of "genocide" is as follows: "killing members of the group; causing serious bodily or mental harm to the group; deliberately inflicting on the group conditions of life calculated to bring about its physical destruction in whole or in part."[4] The ten stages of genocide are classification (creating ethnic divisions), symbolization (coded language to refer to target groups), discrimination (a dominant group denies rights to other groups), dehumanization (one group denies the humanity of the other), organization (the state or perpetrator finds a way to target certain groups), polarization (extremists drive groups apart and silence or kill moderates), preparation (victims are separated into ghettos by ethnic identity and concentrated in prisons or camps), persecution (victims are identified and segregated based on race or religion and then harmed in some way), extermination (killing begins; officials of the state are utilized to round up individuals belonging to certain groups), and denial (perpetrators deny and cover up, usually indicating that more killing is on the way).[5] According to many observers, the United States is in the final two stages of genocide against African Americans, extermination and denial. Under these circumstances, we can have our personal lives or we can have our Christian witness to the world, but we cannot have both. We must therefore die to self in order to be Christ's witnesses.

We must either abolish the prison-industrial complex or stop preaching and sharing the good news about the Christ who said that he came explicitly to release the oppressed. If we continue to preach the gospel and yet fail to actively resist and to stop this genocide, Matthew 25:31-46 offers a special promise for our goat-like hypocrisy: when the hypocrisy goes up, eternal damnation comes down. The only legitimately Christian response to genocide is resistance. To resist, we must face the same evil force that hunted and captured blacks in Africa for the Middle Passage. It has been reinvented within the PIC. The evil force of which we speak is the spirit/ideology of the Great White Hunter.

The Great White Hunter

The African American community has been recaptured and enslaved again by the spirit of the Great White Hunter. In the historical records of eighteenth-century Europe and East Africa the Great White Hunter was the big-game hunter. The big-game hunter traveled to East Africa to hunt elephants and rhinoceroses. This activity was very popular among wealthy Europeans and North Americans during the 1700s. The native people identified them as "white hunters." The white hunters represented the colonizing powers that wanted to create new economies. The colonizers claimed that the unchecked animal population posed a serious threat to their plans, so they had to wipe them out.

Today, the ideological proponents of the Great White Hunter's philosophy regard descendants of African slaves as unchecked, disposable, and suitable for being wiped out. In 2012 a white law-enforcement agent, God-fearing, church-attending Christian, with two young daughters, stood with me in my neighborhood and explained his solution to repeat drug offenders and crime: "My solution is extermination." I said calmly, "How do we do that?" He responded, "Stick a needle in their necks." It is well-documented in the historical literature that African Americans were and are viewed by many as animals.[6] There are also leaders and policy makers in this country who believe that African Americans are like an unchecked licentious animal population threatening the nation's homeland security, an undeserving and lazy ethnic group drawing down federal and state safety net benefits. In 2010 André Bauer, the lieutenant governor of South Carolina at that time, said,

> My grandmother was not a highly educated woman, but she told me as a small child to quit feeding stray animals. . . . You know

why? Because they breed. You're facilitating the problem if you give an animal or a person ample food supply. They will reproduce, especially ones that don't think too much further than that. And so what you've got to do is you've got to curtail that type of behavior. They don't know any better.[7]

In 1924 author Richard Connell published a short story based on the romantic notion of the Great White Hunter searching for big game. In his story, "The Most Dangerous Game," a wealthy aristocrat becomes bored with hunting animals and decides to hunt a human being of the same race who was also a hunter. The human to be hunted was purposely stranded on an island. (In slave narratives you can find photos of white men hunting black men. One wonders if "Niggerhead," the moniker of various geographic features across the U.S., including hunting lands owned by Texas governor and former presidential candidate Rick Perry, originated in such hunting activity by slaveholders.) In 1994, seventy years later, an African American filmmaker, Ernest Dickerson, and an Anglo screenwriter, Eric Bernt, brought Richard Connell's story to life again. This time the hunted human is a black homeless man, played by African American rapper Ice-T. The hunters are five very wealthy men: four white men and a black character playing the role of an "Uncle Tom." The name of the film is *Surviving the Game*. It received bad reviews, and it did poorly at the box office. I was captivated by it in 1994 because the one black hunter and the gratuitous violence needed to get it to the big screen did not totally wipe out its covert message.

Ernest Dickerson is a Howard University graduate who grew up in the projects in Newark, New Jersey. During that time the administration of President Clinton added sixty new felonies punishable by death to the anticrime bill—that is, sixty more ways to kill black and poor people. Ernest Dickerson was warning us that blacks were being hunted by wealthy white aristocrats and by opportunistic black people who think like racist hunters. Seventeen years later blacks are not "surviving the game." There are Great White Hunters on Capitol Hill and in every State assembly.

The Great White Hunter wants a small government. The Great White Hunter wants less government regulation and accountability for big business and the hunt. The Great White Hunter selects his prey carefully. He and his closest friends do the hunting. Presidential candidate Mitt Romney classified the prey in his address to supporters in 2012:

> There are 47 percent of the people who will vote for the president no matter what. All right, there are 47 percent who are with him, who are dependent upon government, who believe that they are victims, who believe the government has a responsibility to care for them, who believe that they are entitled to health care, to food, to housing, to you-name-it. That that's an entitlement. And the government should give it to them. And they will vote for this president no matter what. . . . These are people who pay no income tax . . . . [M]y job is not to worry about those people. I'll never convince them they should take personal responsibility and care for their lives.[8]

The 47 percent are the hunted. The other 53 percent are the hunters and their knowing and unknowing allies. The hunter cannot be identified solely by race. African American presidential candidate Herman Cain seemed to profess similar views. The Great White Hunter is therefore a metaphor for a person of any race who thinks like the big-game hunters of the eighteenth century or the hunters in Ernest Dickerson's remake of Connell's fictional short story.

We must not be fooled by the hunter's camouflage. The Great White Hunter is not trying to fight the terrorists. He is trying to emulate them. Terrorist-dictators have small governments. Terrorist-dictators kill with impunity. Terrorist-dictators allow wealth to be concentrated in the hands of a few friends. Terrorist-dictators refer to peaceful protesters as mobs. Terrorist-dictators say nothing when their allies go to protests wearing assault rifles. Terrorist-dictators trample the civil, human, and legal rights of poor people and those outside of their group.

Open Hunting Season on Blacks and the Poor Must End

What do we do in light of an open hunting season declared on black and poor people? We must change the laws of the land. In order to do so, we will have to appeal to the conscience of Congress.

Therefore, I decided to check the Congressional Bible. The Congressional Bible is the Bible that Great White Hunters like Eric Cantor and John Boehner would keep in their Capitol Hill offices, and a copy of which resides in the Congressional Library. It is the same as your Bible and mine, but it has a seat at the table in Congress. In the fight back, Christians must engage the Great White Hunter on heaven's terms. Encourage them to open their Congressional Bibles and to read passages about poor people. For those who claim to be Christians, remind them of who they are in Christ. They either will be won over by their own faith, or they will be forced to renounce their faith and pledge allegiance to the false gods that have led them astray.

It appears that hunters on Capitol Hill do not agree with their Congressional Bible. Their Bible said, "If you offer your food to the hungry and satisfy the needs of the afflicted, then your light shall rise in the darkness" (Isaiah 58:10 NRSV). Their Bible said, "If you want to repent and to bear good fruit, then whoever has two coats must share with anyone who has none; and whoever has food must do likewise" (Luke 3:8, 11 NRSV [adapted]). The leader of the Congressional Bible, a colored boy named "Jesus," offered quality health care to the rich and the poor regardless of preexisting conditions like sin. The Congressional Bible says, "From everyone who has been given much, much will be demanded" (Luke 12:48 NIV). The Great White Hunters in Congress oppose policies that accomplish these aims.

Vocal artist Kanye West once said that George Bush didn't care about black people. It is worse than that. The friends of George Bush whom he left in power hate black and poor people. If I were visiting from another universe, after an examination of the allocation of resources and the administration of jurisprudence, I would have to conclude that the government of the United States of America hates poor people.

What Jesus Told His Disciples to Do

In the Congressional Bible, at John 20:19, we find that it is open season on people who loved Jesus. They were being hunted by officials. The disciples were like many of us after the extermination of Troy Davis, Trayvon Martin, Jonathan Ferrell, Renisha McBride,

Eric Garner, and Mike Brown—huddled together, dismayed, contemplating the fate of the community from this point forward. As the disciples were calculating their fate, Jesus appeared and stood among them. The message that Jesus brought to them is a message for any Christian who accepts the realty of black genocide in the United States of America.

Here's the situation. The disciples are gathered in a room behind locked doors. The doors are locked because the disciples are afraid of the Jewish authorities. If you hang out with a convicted criminal, there is a pretty good chance that the authorities will identify you as a troublemaker too. The disciples were on the most-wanted list. The authorities could not allow twelve more men, one by one, to claim that they had kingdoms not of this world, or that they were one with God, or had the power to forgive sins. Therefore, the disciples went into hiding. They were trying to figure out their next move when Jesus came and stood among them behind locked doors.

If you had just witnessed an execution, and the man you saw executed appeared behind locked doors, there might be some spontaneous profanity, screaming, grabbing of the head, crying, running to the opposite side of the room and passing out. If Troy Davis walked into your room right now as you read this article, would you not lose your mind? This must have been the case for the disciples too, because the first thing Jesus has to say is "Peace be with you" (John 20:19).

Peter is there. A week earlier Peter had pulled out a sword and cut off a man's ear. One wonders if hot-tempered Peter tried to tackle the risen imposter. The author of the Gospel of John left these details out. Or, perhaps he does not have time for those kinds of details; he has to tell us what truly matters for all eternity. As readers of the Gospel, we are in shock by what we are reading, just as the disciples must have been in shock. Nonetheless, the Gospel of John goes straight to the next thing that Jesus does. Jesus shows them his hands and sides, as if to say, "Yeah, it's really me. You saw what you saw. Yes, they killed me. It really happened." Then, after proving that he was indeed their friend who was executed, while the disciples must have been saying, "Shhhh! Hold it down before five-o finds us," Jesus has the nerve to show off his scars and say to them, "As the Father sent me, so I am sending you" (John 20:21).

Here's what I might have said in reply: "Really, Jesus, are you kidding? Pump your brakes, son of Mary. *You* claimed to be the son of God. Not me." As I read this text, I think that if I were Peter, I would have denied Jesus a fourth time and taken the next ship to Greece. Yet, things are happening too rapidly. Jesus did not waste a moment. The Congressional Bible says, "Then Jesus breathed on them and said, 'Receive the Holy Spirit. If you forgive anyone's sins, they are forgiven. If you do not forgive them, they are not forgiven'" (John 20:22-23).

Jesus appeared and stood among disciples, who were afraid, in hiding, unprepared to survive the Christian hunting season. Jesus' message for us is the same: "Be at peace, do not hide, I will give you my Spirit to equip you to fight the fight."

Jesus' response to fear was "Peace be with you." When we are being hunted and persecuted, the most dangerous thing for us is to become paralyzed by fear. When paralyzed, we are easy targets. It is the deer that keeps moving, the bird that swoops down behind a tree, the bear that zigzags through the forest that escapes the hunter. Jesus' appearance to the disciples after his execution demonstrates that God is in control of the hunt. "Peace be with you." In other words, Jesus was saying, "I know that things look grim. I know that you are being chased down by the authorities. However, you need to know that there is no Jewish authority, no court system, no armed guard, no tribulation, no prison cell, no military action beyond my Father's control."

Next, he said to his undercover, stowaway, following-Jesus-on-the-down-low disciples, "As the Father sent me, so I send you." We should be mystified by Jesus' single-mindedness. In the aftermath of a hurricane created by Jesus' radical message, gruesome death, and spellbinding resurrection, he said to the disciples, "You'd better get going. Get your things together. You don't have to go home, but you can't hide out here." In the face of genocide, Jesus needs us to understand that we cannot hide from our own persecution. Jesus was saying to the disciples, "It's your turn to make some trouble."

No Christian should make it through this life without getting into some kind of trouble for Jesus. If Jesus is the light *of* the world, then his followers are lights *in* the world. We know what light does. Light always fights back the evil. Light has something to say and do about one in nine young black men and one in one hundred black women in their thirties being in prison. The light has something to say about the New Jim Crow, which legalizes discrimination against people with records.[9] The light has something to say about millions of indigent people being bullied into pleading guilty to crimes that they did not commit in order to avoid outrageous prison sentences. An encounter with the risen Christ moves us away from isolation and denial toward troublemaking.

The tactic of evil forces, human and spiritual, is to isolate believers in hiding so that they can be plucked off one by one. A good hunter will get big game to separate from the pack and then, one by one, will take them out. There is no victory in working alone. There is no victory in an isolated hideout. To know God is to stand in unity and to look a threat in the face and say, "And? What?! Bring it!"

Lastly, the disciples were unprepared to take action. So Jesus equipped them. "Then he breathed on them and said, 'Receive the Holy Spirit.'" When the Holy Spirit is involved, believers are fully equipped in the hunting season. The Holy Spirit is essential to the fight. Without the Holy Spirit we may begin to hate our enemies. Without the Holy Spirit we risk losing respect for the humanity of others. The minute we forget how to forgive and be gracious, we lose the fight. With the indwelling of the Holy Spirit comes divine power to resist the hunter, to love the hunter, to continue to dialogue with the hunter, and to pray for the people hunting us down. In 2 Peter 1:3-4 it is said this way: "His divine power has given us everything needed for life and godliness . . . so that through them you may escape the corruption that is in the world because of lust, and may become participants of the divine nature" (NRSV). The Holy Spirit equips us to shelter the prey from the predators. We will need more miracles in the resistance and effort to abolish prisons and end this genocide. More miracles, however, require a shift in perspective.

We should not be asking for miracles. Too many of us have been Christians long enough to stop going to God in prayer with our hands out. When we read Scripture, it is a mistake for a mature Christian to identify with the people who came to Jesus only to fill a need, to be freed from sin, or to be healed of sickness. It is a mistake to continue to identify with the masses of people in the Gospels who ate from his table but who were not about his business. After Jesus' execution the disciples were still in line for a miracle. But I want to remind the reader of what Jesus said to the disciples after his execution: "Be at peace, do not hide, the Holy Spirit will equip you." It may look like we need a miracle right now, but if we are in line for a miracle, we are in the wrong line. You, the reader, are the miracle. You have power to manifest miracles in the courtroom, in the bond hearing room, in the prison room, and in the Congressional room.

The classic Shirley Caesar song "You're Next in Line for a Miracle" is good if you are the man who has been sick for thirty-eight years (John 5); it is good if you are the hungry five thousand whom Jesus fed (John 6); it is good if you are the woman about to be stoned (John 8). But when you become a disciple of Christ, things change. After we get a few miracles of our own, we are not supposed to be in the miracle receiving line anymore.

The masses are still waiting for God's liberating and genocide-ending power to be made manifest because too many of us are in the wrong line. There are not enough miracles because we are waiting for them instead of performing them. There are not enough miracles in this open season because we are not in the line where miracles are *performed*. Miracles are not performed in the miracle receiving line. *Miracles are performed in the line for crucifixions.* Dear reader and disciple of Christ, you are *not* next in line for a miracle. "As the Father sent me, so I send you," said Jesus, which means, "You are next in line for a crucifixion."

We will not have any problem finding the line for crucifixions. Just look for lines of Christians, and then pick the shortest line. Look for the line with the most women in it. Look for the line with the most black men in it. Look for the line with the most poor people in it. Look for the line of people occupying the prisons. Look for the line of people holding a vigil near an execution. It seems like the people who have been persecuted the most catch on to the gospel the quickest. When we make it to the front of the line, we will get a cross. After we carry that cross, we will have to get back in line again, and carry another cross. And after we carry that cross, we will have to get in line again, and carry another cross. We just keep on doing that until we are actually executed, or we go home to the Lord knowing that we were in the right line.

Temptations will come. If we look over to the miracle-receiving line, we may think, "My God, those Christians in the miracle-receiving line look awfully happy. Their Jesus requires little of them. He gives away cars and houses." Do not be fooled, dear reader. If you do something, and God is *required* to act, that is not faith; that is superstition. If you believe that God gives miracles on demand, throw away your Bible and get a crystal ball. There are no miracles on demand. Instead, we must find our peace in the midst of fear. Get out from behind locked doors and connect with others with Holy Spirit power. Jesus says, "Very truly, I tell you, the one who believes in me will also do the works that I do and, in fact, will do greater works than these, because I am going to the Father" (John 14:12 NRSV).

Faith with Works Is Alive

There is indeed a Great Hunter; but he is not white, and he is not black. This Hunter is the Alpha and Omega of all hunters. Those of us who make God an enemy cannot hide behind "tough on crime" legislation or permit genocide to continue unchecked. God will hunt us down in this life or the next. Nothing will cover up our scent. Forget your bulletproof vest, it will not work.

With spiritual eyes, I see the camouflage of a different kind of Hunter coming to our aid. I see the orange safety jacket and the loaded wrath of a Hunter whose big game is injustice. This Hunter stalks poverty. This Hunter preys upon the greedy. This Hunter lays a trap for the arrogant. This Hunter puts the face of the oppressor in his crosshairs. Oh, the Greatest Hunter of Hunters has spoken clearly to believers, "Be at peace, do not hide. My Spirit is with you. As the Father sent me, so I send you. You're next in line for a crucifixion."

The credibility of every Christian hangs in the balance as long as the prison-industrial complex enjoys a peaceful coexistence with believers. To reform the PIC rather than dismantle it is complicity. Would you have been satisfied with slavery if it were simply reformed? One cannot reform genocide; it must be abolished. The PIC is too big and corrupt for reform. The replacement system is a restorative-justice system. This is what biblical law ordains. When we wrong someone, we make it right (see Leviticus 5–6; 17). Atonement and redemption can occur in the community without imprisoning youth and poor minorities. We have numerous community alternatives to imprisonment in effect today in this country. Restorative justice must become the law of the land, or else criminal justice will destroy our communities and nation and waste our resources. Those who are dangerous should be contained in a mental health facility, not a cage. However, the cage, even if comparable to a Martha Stewart–styled room, is still a cage.[10] No reflection of the divine nature should be kept in a cage. No human being should be targeted, profiled, hunted down, captured, and stripped away from his or her family. But this is happening to our neighbors this very moment. We must do something. If we don't, we must renounce our baptism and stop preaching the gospel.

Questions for Consideration

1. If you were completely unchained, what would you do for the kingdom?
2. Given what you have read, are you willing to fight to abolish prisons? Why? Why not?
3. If a Christian person is not willing to fight to abolish prisons, should he/she be required to renounce his/her baptism? Why? Why not?

Notes

1. See "What Works," a synopsis of the findings of criminal psychologist D. A. Andrews of Carleton University (http://exodusfoundation.org/sample-page/understanding-the-issues/what-works/).

2. Jenifer Warren, et al., "One in 100: Behind Bars in America 2008," published by The Pew Charitable Trust (http://www.colorado.gov/ccjjdir/Resources/Resources/Ref/PEW_OneIn100.pdf).

3. Children's Defense Fund, "Cradle to Prison Pipeline Fact Sheet," October 2009 (http://www.childrensdefense.org/child-research-data-publications/data/cradle-to-prison-pipeline-overview-fact-sheet-2009.pdf).

4. "Convention on the Prevention and Punishment of the Crime of Genocide," adopted by Resolution 260 (III) A of the United Nations General Assembly on December 9, 1948 (https://treaties.un.org/doc/Publication/UNTS/Volume%2078/volume-78-I-1021-English.pdf).

5. Gregory H. Stanton, "The 10 Stages of Genocide," *Genocide Watch* (http://genocidewatch.org/genocide/tenstagesofgenocide.html).

6. H. Shelton Smith, *In His Image, But . . . : Racism in Southern Religion, 1780–1910* (Durham, NC: Duke University Press, 1972). See also William Lee Miller, *Arguing about Slavery: John Quincy Adams and the Great Battle in the United States Congress* (New York: Vintage Books, 1995); Douglas A. Blackmon, *Slavery by Another Name: The Re-Enslavement of Black Americans from the Civil War to World War II* (New York: Doubleday, 2008).

7. Brian Montopoli, "S.C. Lt. Gov. André Bauer Compares Helping Poor to Feeding Stray Animals," CBS News, January 25, 2010 (http://www.cbsnews.com/news/sc-lt-gov-andre-bauer-compares-helping-poor-to-feeding-stray-animals/). This quotation is demonstrative of the rhetoric directed against food stamps and health care that dominates public policy discussions. The term "poor" has been code for "African Americans" and other already disliked people since the early 1980s. See Martin Gilens, "How the Poor Became Black: The Racialization of American Poverty in the Mass Media" in *Race and the Politics of Welfare Reform*, ed. Sanford F. Schram, Joe Soss and Richard C. Fording (Detroit: University of Michigan Press, 2003), 101–30.

8. David Corn, "Mitt Romney's Incredible 47-Percent Denial: 'Actually, I Didn't Say That,'" *Mother Jones*, July 29, 2013 (http://www.motherjones.com/mojo/2013/07/mitt-romney-47-percent-denial).

9. An absolutely indispensable resource for abolitionists is Michelle Alexander, *The New Jim Crow: Mass Incarceration in the Age of Colorblindness* (New York: New Press, 2010).

10. See Mark Morris, ed., *Instead of Prisons: A Handbook for Abolitionists* (Syracuse, NY: Prison Research Education Action Project, 1976).

10

break CAMP

Becoming a Church on Purpose with Purpose for Purpose

REGINALD W. WILLIAMS JR.

THE CHICAGO BEARS HAVE THEIR PRESEASON CAMP JUST A FEW miles from our church at Olivet Nazarene University. They have been training there for the past 13 years, three intense and highly competitive weeks in the heat of the summer. But every August, the training ends. They have learned the plays; they have absorbed the strategies drilled by the coaches. They have survived the grueling physical conditioning, practicing in all weather. But finally, the prep work is done. And the technical term the team uses to indicate that training camp has come to an end is "Break camp."

In the New International Version's translation of Deuteronomy 1:6, the Scripture says, "The LORD our God said to us at Horeb, 'You have stayed long enough at this mountain. Break camp....'" That may not seem like much to you—just one verse in a long and detailed biblical book of narrative and laws. But that's a mouthful, because of who is speaking and because of what is said.

Listen

In the New Revised Standard Version, the text says, "The LORD our God *spoke*." There is something powerful when God speaks. In the beginning, God spoke and chaos became cosmos. That's power.

When God spoke into that original chaos, darkness gave way to light. When God spoke to the formless void, the world came into being. That's the power of Creation. And God's word has the ability to create something from nothing every time the Lord speaks.

God is speaking, I wonder, are we listening? What does God have to say about the way we treat the environment, and the way we treat our bodies, and the way we treat each other? I wonder what God is saying in the midst of all of this tragedy that is nagging our nation and plaguing our planet?

This Scripture says, "The Lord God spoke to us!" The fact that God speaks to God's people, to us, is a gift of grace. And ever since that first divine word gave birth to creation, God has spoken to God's people in specific contexts, at specific times and in specific locations. And sometimes, location is everything.

Location

In this particular Scripture, the Lord spoke to the people at Horeb. Now, Horeb was the location where Moses received the Ten Commandments. This was the place where the constitution and covenant of Creator and creation was commenced, communicated, and consummated. This was the location, Horeb, the mountain of God where the people were to get the law and move toward their destiny. *This was the location.*

Don't get me wrong. Horeb was a location where God's people had great memories. Forty years ago, Horeb had been a literal mountaintop experience. But, Horeb was not—then or now—their final destination. They were on their way to Kadesh Barnea, but they stopped at Horeb. It was a pit stop, really. They were supposed to continue on, but they stopped at Horeb and got stuck where they stopped.

Deuteronomy 1:2 helps us to see the problem. The problem is that the law was given to the people forty years ago. And it should have taken roughly eleven days to get from the location where they were (Horeb) to the destination where they were going (the Promised Land). And yet, here they were, forty years later, back in the same place after forty years of wandering—and apparently they were prepared to settle in for a long stay!

Church, we have the tendency to linger too long in locations that we probably should have left. We may have some amazing history there. We may have some impressive altars and some even more impressive memories. Israel certainly did! But God spoke to them in that place and said, "Enough. You've been on the mountain long enough. It's time to move on." But because they had gotten stuck where they stopped, instead of stepping, they settled because they didn't realize their location. They didn't realize that they had lingered too long. They still didn't realize that their current location was not their final destination.

I was at the airport recently. As I boarded the plane, I saw another man who was trying to get on but the officials wouldn't allow him. He was flying standby. And he had to stand by because he had been booked on an earlier flight. He was in the airport on a layover, but he had missed his connection. How did that happen? It wasn't that his incoming flight had been delayed. It wasn't because he lost his luggage. It wasn't for any reason but that he was not paying attention to the time when he should have been boarding. When they called his flight (several times!), he was not listening. When they paged him by name over the loud speaker, he was not listening. He was at one of the airport restaurants, watching TV, eating, and drinking, as if he had nowhere else to be and nowhere else to go. He missed his flight because he treated his layover as though it was his final destination.

There are some locations where God's people ought not to linger too long. Because if we linger too long, we just may get left behind and never arrive where we are meant to be. Church, if we're going to reach our final destination, we have to listen. We have to realize our location. And we have to recognize when it's time to leave.

Leave

Sometimes, I don't think we understand what leaving means. Leaving has a very deep yet simple definition to it. I did my research, and found out that leaving means *not staying where you are*. That's what God told the people of Israel. The Scripture says, God told the Israelites, "You have stayed long enough at this mountain. Resume your journey." In other words, God told them, it's time to leave. They were stuck in a place that was supposed to be a pit stop. And

I want to suggest that the Christian church today has gotten stuck in much the same way.

People of God, it's time to break camp. Break camp in how we do education and evangelism. Break camp in how we preach and teach. Break camp in how we understand Jesus and justice. The church too often holds on to traditions for the sake of holding on to traditions, with the hard reality being that some churches would rather die holding on to traditions, than break camp and grow being faithful to the God of the church. And God could be saying to us as the church that it's time to BREAK CAMP. This is not your final destination.

So, this word to God's people at Horeb is a word for us today. Church, we have to leave our Mt. Horeb if we're ever going to get to where God's call is going. In order to get to where God would have us, sometimes we have to leave.

That's what God told Israel. And that's what God is telling the church today. That's what the voices of these awesome authors and excellent editors in this volume have been proclaiming. It's time to listen, to recognize our location, and to realize that where we are isn't where we're meant to be. This isn't our final destination. As a church, we need to break camp from the old and antiquated ways of doing and being church because we've been there too long. And I'm not just talking about the church you attend. I'm talking about the Church Universal, the Body of Christ in the world!

Destination: Justice

So, what is our destination? It has to do with pursuit of justice (Micah 6:8). The church must not confuse charity and justice any longer. Consider this illustration to exemplify the concept. Have you ever heard someone talk about the difference between a thermostat and a thermometer? The thermometer changes in response to the temperature around it; it is merely an instrument that reacts to its environment. In contrast, a thermostat *changes* the temperature of the environment surrounding it. The environment responds to the action of the thermostat: Too cold? Thermostat turns on the furnace and the environment warms up. Too hot? Thermostat activates the air conditioning and the room cools off.

Too often in the history of the church, our ministry in the world has been more like a thermometer than a thermostat. We have been quick to engage ministries of charity, of compassion and care, which like the thermometer, are reactions to the world around us. Charity reacts to real needs, but it does so after the damage is done. When the economy shifts downward, more soup kitchens open because of the increase in the homeless population and unemployment rates.

However, charity is meant to be a way station, a pit stop, a temporary reprieve. It is meant to be Mt. Horeb—and the church ought to be breaking camp to move on. We need to pass through the thermometer phase of ministry and into a thermostat mode of action. Justice ministries, like a thermostat, seek to change the environment itself. Justice is proactive. Justice seeks to eliminate the need for soup kitchens in the first place. Justice work places pressure on politicians and policy makers to ensure that none of God's children are too hot from the heat of oppressive measures or too cold from the wintry fingers of political and societal rejection. Justice work seeks to balance the temperature, and not just reflect the temperature as it is.

Archbishop Dom Hélder Câmara brought both of these separate, yet, related themes to bear when he observed, "When I give food to the poor, they call me a saint. When I ask why the poor have no food, they call me a communist."[1]

The archbishop's concern is valid today. Oppressors are comfortable with charitable organizations and individuals. People in power do not mind having those in need assisted. However, when the work of justice challenges the systems that make charity necessary, problems arise. Challenging the systems challenges the privilege and power of those who don't mind throwing a few crumbs of charity, but who refuse to establish systems of equality, mutuality, reciprocity, and impartiality.

I'm not suggesting that the church abandon our ministries of charity; our compassionate and caring service is vital in a world that is suffering. But we dare not stay camped there. We must remember that both charity and justice are essential to the work we do as the Body of Christ on earth.

The truth of the matter is that sometimes, the focus on charity only impedes progress toward justice—for the givers as well as the receivers of such charity. Charity can cause people to accept things as they are and never seek to break camp. It can blind us to the need to seek the change that justice provides so that charity will not be necessary. However, until the day comes where charity is not necessary, there must be an interlocked, concerted effort, that includes charity and justice! In the world in which we live, we do not have the luxury of forsaking justice for charity, or charity for justice. We must employ both in order to bring about a world where God's people will be treated as God would have them be treated. Maybe God is moving us to move exclusively out of being charity-minded to being justice-motivated!

As a community, maybe God is telling us to break camp. In the words of Dr. Martin Luther King, no longer can we expect freedom and liberation to be given by the oppressor; it must be demanded by the oppressed. No longer can we assimilate and allow others to control the economics in our community. No longer can we expect others to think for us and do what's in our best interest. No longer can we expect others to do for us what we can do for ourselves. Church, no longer can we expect seekers to come to us; they are already in the world, working for justice, serving the suffering in compassion and care. It's time for us to get out of our pews, out of our church buildings, and join them. Maybe God is telling us as a community of faith that we've got to break camp.

In our personal conditions, our churches, our communities, and our country, in our comfortable conditions wherever we may be, God is telling us that it's time to break camp.

Moments into Movement

Look again at the Scripture. The moment came when God broke through the people's comfort zone and told them "You've been here long enough." That was the moment. But in order for them to get to where they were going, that moment had to become the impetus for their movement. They would never get to where they were going, had that moment not pushed them to some kind of movement. And I believe that, in our lives, there are moments God uses that push us to movements.

The Church on Purpose must engage in a movement to erase racism. Unarmed black men shot, like Trayvon Martin and Michael Brown, or choked in the streets, like Eric Garner, or executed without evidence of guilt, like Troy Davis. Injured black women, like

Renisha McBride, shot down while seeking help in a fearful white neighborhood.

The Church on Purpose must engage in movement to erase sexism. Women, still making less money than men for doing the same jobs.

The Church on Purpose must also engage in movement to erase militarism. Occupying lands for the sake of preserving Empire, while decimating others who may be different from us.

The Church on Purpose must engage in movement to erase heterosexism. Discrimination against someone based on who they are and whom they love. This is the moment for the Church on Purpose to end these transgressions against another's humanity.

Author Victor Hugo said, "If the soul is left in darkness, sins will be committed. The guilty one is not he who commits the sin, but he who causes the darkness."[2] And too many people benefit from the darkness they caused with the structural and institutional, oppressive and repressive policies put in place. Structural and institutional oppression, in all of its varied forms, is in the very foundational fabric of this country. And the only way that structural and institutional oppression can be undermined is by people deciding that they will BREAK CAMP and engage in a movement.

What does God have to say about a place like University Park, Illinois, where there is a golf course but nowhere to get good groceries? What does God have to say about the U.S.-supported terror being rained down in Gaza and Palestine? What does God have to say about Ferguson, and the many "Fergusons" around the country and the world? What does God have to say about the flooding of our neighborhoods with guns? What does God have to say about the greed that is economically paralyzing our communities? What does God have to say about how we are treating the environment? What does God have to say about how we treat LGBTQ brothers and sisters? What does God have to say about the deafening silence of the church on matters of oppression, depression, and repression?

We have so many moments but don't have a movement. When will we break camp out of moments, and become a movement? Movements don't have photo opportunities as a main goal. Movements don't need to be seen on television. Movements require that each and every day we get up and do the work of justice and liberation for all of God's children. If our moments don't turn into movements, we will stay miserable.

This moment when God spoke to the people of Israel—it turned into a movement. The people listened to the word of the Lord. They looked around and realized their location was only meant to be a layover. And then they gathered the courage to leave. Church, the same can be true for us. Because if we listen and realize location and dare to leave, then our moments can turn into movements. If you don't believe me, just consider history.

Many people think it was Rosa Park's defiant stand by sitting down that started the Civil Rights Movement. And that was a heck of a moment, because that moment kicked off the Montgomery bus boycott. But there was another moment back in August 1955 when a 13-year-old boy was killed by some insecure men and dropped in the Tallahatchie River. And the rebellious Rosa Parks said that, when she sat down, she was thinking about Emmitt Till's body as it was courageously shown to the world.

I will say it again. God is speaking. Are we listening? I wonder what God is saying in the midst of all of this tragedy that is nagging our nation and plaguing our planet?

When I take time to listen, it seems to me that God is issuing a challenge to the church. I hear the Lord saying, "It's time to break camp!" We cannot afford to do church like we've always done church. If you are listening, then break camp, and expand your ideas of evangelism. Listen for different models of leadership that empower and don't devour. Break camp, and institute some revolutionary ways of faith formation that help people deal with politics, money, and sex. Break camp, and dare to engage in revolutionary discipleship, to cultivate creative community, and to follow the Jesus of justice.

Break camp, church! We cannot afford to stick our heads in the sand, and refuse to address the societal ills that call out for justice, in the name of a pietistic and ritualistic religion. If we are going to be *Church on Purpose*, then we need to break camp. Seems as though God is saying to the people in the Scripture and in our time, *BREAK CAMP!*

Notes

1. http://www.goodreads.com/quotes/show/20321 (accessed January 29, 2015).
2. https://www.goodreads.com/author/quotes/13661.Victor_Hugo (accessed January 29, 2015).